Living Deliberately
Experiments in
Practical Spirituality

John H. McMurphy, Ph.D.

Amaranth Publishing

Living Deliberately
Experiments in
Practical Spirituality

John H. McMurphy, Ph.D.

Published by:

 Amaranth Publishing
P.O. Box 764167
Dallas, TX 75376

ISBN 0-9635487-8-6

Cover Art by Ryan Thrash Designs in Dallas

For information on John McMurphy's workshops, please call toll–free in the U.S. & Canada: (800) 321–2760

— Acknowledgments —

I wish to acknowledge people whose efforts have been instrumental in writing this book. First, Jeffrey Davis demonstrated extraordinary sensitivity to Thoreau's ideas as he diligently edited my work. His suggestions for expressing Thoreau's message have been an invaluable resource for communicating timeless wisdom to a contemporary audience.

I also would like to thank King Butler, a former student of mine at Southern Methodist University, for his efforts in helping me assemble the fruits of several years research into Thoreau's life into this book. It is a joy to find young people who realize that humanity can live more deliberately through a conscious endeavor.

Thoreau — an eternal presence

Finally, I acknowledge Henry Thoreau, the primary inspiration for this book. My immersion in his *Journals* and his life has helped me to see that "great minds" never really leave us. They remain an active and vital force for all who have eyes and ears for their message. To me, Thoreau is as alive as ever, because his spirit is an eternal one. His determination to live deliberately in his own lifetime has created patterns in human consciousness that we can access and use today in our own efforts to live more deliberately. The insights in this book from contemporary thinkers such as Ernest Holmes and Carl Jung confirm Thoreau's insights, as do the practices of Native Americans. These people have applied spiritual principles in their daily activities in order to live more deliberately. They will be our guides for the experiments in practical spirituality.

CONTENTS

PART ONE:
THOREAU, WHY NOW?

PART TWO:
EXPERIMENTS IN
PRACTICAL SPIRITUALITY

SUGGESTIONS FOR USING THIS BOOK

There are many biographies of Henry Thoreau, the primary inspiration for this book. To my knowledge, however, there are no books that incorporate his ideas with experiments in practical spirituality that will help us do as he advises us—*to live deliberately.* There also are no books, to my knowledge, that unite insights and activities from Thoreau, Native Americans, Ernest Holmes, Carl Jung, and other great minds on the subject of living deliberately. As this book's approach to practical spirituality is somewhat unique, please use the following suggestions as a guide.

• **"All life is an experiment, the more experiments, the better" wrote Thoreau's friend Ralph Waldo Emerson** — Thoreau certainly took his friend's advice to heart, for his life became a remarkable experiment in living deliberately. *Failure* does not exist for people committed to experimentation, because they know they always can learn something from their experiments—even if they did not get the results they had expected or desired. Please keep Emerson's advice in mind as you conduct the experiments in Part Two.

• **You are part of the process** — Rather than spelling out in detail the potential meaning of Thoreau's ideas, I have prepared only a small opening remark on each of his main themes such as Nature, friendship, and human nature. This gives you the freedom to construct the meaning of his ideas *in your own terms* through reading, contemplation, and keeping a journal. It also places the responsibility for discovering Thoreau's message upon you, which is what I feel Thoreau would want. The more actively you engage yourself in the learning process, the greater will be your potential benefit.

• **The techniques and exercises in Part Two will provide inspiration**— Many techniques and exercises actually used by Thoreau, other great minds, and Native Americans are included in Part Two. Practicing these activities will help integrate spiritual principles into your daily life. *The goal is to learn by doing.*

• **Proceeding slowly enhances your experience** — There is no need to rush through this text. Moving slowly through each section and allowing it to blossom in your mind is more beneficial than completing it quickly. Spending a day exploring a quotation or the results from an experiment could be an appropriate way to progress through the book. Let your intuitive wisdom guide your progress. *Whenever you feel that you have discovered what a quotation or an experiment has to offer, then proceed.*

• **Record your thoughts in a journal to promote understanding** — Great minds such as Thoreau kept journals, and so must we — *if we desire to understand their wisdom.* The journal will be your greatest ally as you explore the ideas and experiments in practical spirituality. If you need assistance with keeping a journal, refer to the exercise in *Experiments in Living Deliberately.*

PART ONE:
Insights on Living Deliberately from Henry Thoreau

"Let me forever go in search of myself; never for a moment think that I have found myself; be as a stranger to myself, never a familiar."

Thoreau, *Journals*

Many people have sought to live deliberately, to find practical applications for spiritual principles. Very few have been as diligent as has Thoreau. He not only thought about living deliberately, but he also conducted numerous experiments in such a lifestyle. He took nothing for granted—not even himself. Everything was part of a grand experiment to discover what it means to be a human being.

Thoreau's search for practical spirituality forms the foundation of this book. In Part Two, insights and activities from Native Americans and contemporary thinkers such as Ernest Holmes and Carl Jung complement Thoreau's ideas.

PREVIEW OF THOREAU'S INSIGHTS

- **Major Events in Thoreau's Life and Era**
- **Thoreau, Why Now?**
- **Thoreau on Himself**
- **True Friendship: Thoreau and Emerson**
- **Thoreau on Human Nature**
- **Thoreau on Nature**

MAJOR EVENTS OF THOREAU'S LIFE

1817   Born on July 12 in Concord, Massachusetts

1833   Enters Harvard where he is an average scholar and a member of the debating society

1836   Reads Emerson's book *Nature* which has a profound effect upon him

1837   Graduates from Harvard; his graduation paper challenges the commercial mindset of his day and is a premonition of his later ideas in *Walden*; he returns to Concord to teach school, but he is dismissed for refusing to administer corporal punishment; meets Emerson who encourages him to keep a journal; their friendship begins to blossom

1838   He and his brother John open a private school; he presents his first lecture before the Concord Lyceum with only modest success; Emerson begins to introduce him into the budding Transcendental Movement and encourages him to write essays

1839   Two week excursion upon the Concord and Merrimack rivers with his brother John; his journal of the experience later evolves into a book

1840	The *Dial*, the Transcendental journal in which Emerson, Bronson Alcott, and Margaret Fuller played prominent roles, publishes one of his essays
1842	His brother John dies; Thoreau grieves at this tremendous loss, and later, he would weep at the mere mention of John's name
1843	Embarks for an extended visit to Staten Island to tutor Emerson's nephew; he maintains an active correspondence with Emerson and writes several poems and essays for the *Dial*
1844	Returns to Concord and resumes his residency in the Emerson household
1845	July 4, takes up residence on Emerson's land beside Walden Pond to begin his experiment in living deliberately
1846	Thoreau is jailed for not paying his local property taxes, because he felt they would contribute to the war with Mexico, a war he opposed on moral grounds; the story goes that Emerson visited Thoreau while he was in jail and said: "Henry, what are you doing in there?" to which Thoreau responded assertively, "Ralph, what are you doing *out there*?"; who actually paid his taxes so he could be released remains a mystery, although many people suspect that it was Emerson

1847	Having concluded his experiment in living deliberately, Thoreau leaves Walden Pond on September 6; he returns to live with Emerson and begins writing *Walden* as a summary of what he had learned from the experiment
1848	Nathaniel Hawthorne, corresponding secretary for the Salem Lyceum, invites Thoreau to present a lecture to the group; he delivers a message drawn from his experiences at Walden Pond; the Salem paper praises his work for being "a strong undercurrent of delicate satire against the follies of our times"; in the years ahead, Thoreau would receive several other invitations to speak about his Walden experience.
1849	Publishes *A Week on the Concord and Merrimack Rivers* and his provocative essay, "Civil Disobedience"
1854	Publishes *Walden*; delivers the stirring address "Slavery in Massachusetts" which stimulates Abolitionist sentiments
1856	Meets Walt Whitman in New York; they strike up an immediate interest in each other's work
1857	Meets John Brown who is visiting Concord to raise money for his anti–slavery efforts; Thoreau is moved by Brown's sincerity and commitment to the Abolitionist cause

1859   Brown again visits Concord and Thoreau delivers the address "Plea for Captain John Brown" at the town hall; his impassioned message stirs many people to become active crusaders in the anti–slavery cause; Thoreau does not endorse Brown's violent acts that were intended to disrupt the business of slavery; instead, he praises Brown's courage for giving his life in support of his principles

1861   In May, Thoreau leaves for Minnesota to recover from bronchitis; unable to recover, he returns to Concord, and accepting his fate, begins to assemble many of his unpublished manuscripts for publication; When his aunt asks him if he had made peace with God, Thoreau replied that he didn't know that he and God had ever quarreled

1862   May 6, 1862 Thoreau dies; his last words — "moose" and "Indian" — reflect his concern for the *Maine Woods* manuscript on which he had been working immediately prior to his death

THOREAU, WHY NOW?

"Today Thoreau is widely rated as one of the giants in the American pantheon and his fame is on an upward rather than a downward curve. It is usually agreed that he speaks more to our day than to his own."

Walter Harding, *The Days of Henry Thoreau*

Harding, one of Thoreau's most prominent biographers, suggests that Thoreau may be a prophet. Prophets, because their eyes and their minds are focused upon the Universal Realm, may appear to be out of step with their own historical era and its inhabitants. Prophets also have a message they feel compelled to deliver, messages that often fall upon deaf ears in the short term, but ultimately may be discovered once humanity has sufficient perspective upon the message. Thoreau meets this description of a prophet, for his writing often displays both distaste for the human predicament in his own day and several profound messages that appear to be appropriate for audiences today.

One of Thoreau's prophetic messages in *Walden* is that humanity must cultivate a spiritual rebirth including what he called "a re–alliance with Nature" if we are to endure. Certainly humanity has made substantive progress in our long journey from "darker" times; however, this has been primarily material progress. In our desire to live more comfortably than our ancestors and to enhance the quality of our lives, we have shortened the work week to create more leisure time. Unfortunately, rather than using this newly available time for developing our spiritual potential which certainly would improve the quality of our lives, we have "invested" our leisure time in the pursuit of additional material comforts and conveniences. We even have become so obsessed with protecting our material treasures and comfortable lifestyle that we have built incredible nuclear arsenals and turned our homes into well–armed fortresses.

Thoreau gave us a "wake–up call"

Thoreau intuited where humanity was headed. Granted, he may not have known that we would create specific "convenience–monsters" such as microwave ovens, disposable diapers, cellular telephones, self–diagnostic dishwashers *ad infinitum* or that we would need "peace-keeper" missiles to protect our materialistic bounty. He did realize, however, that our addiction to material pleasures as a means of determining the quality of our lives would ultimately lead us to disaster, just as we finally are discovering. His message in *Walden's* opening was that his experiment in living simply and deliberately beside Walden Pond would be humanity's "wake–up call." Many people today already have begun to heed his advice that we redirect our path towards spiritual qualities in lieu of seeking materialistic gratification. Others will follow.

Shortly after completing his Walden Pond experiment in living deliberately, Thoreau posited another powerful message to contemporary generations in his essay "Civil Disobedience." His clear, eloquent premise that it is far more honorable to disobey a law that shows contempt for the value of human life than it is to obey such a law has changed reality in this century.

Gandhi, Martin Luther King, Bishop Desmond Tutu, Danish resisters to the Germans during World War Two, and many others who have given of themselves—even if it meant going to prison or being killed—in the struggle for human rights have proclaimed that Thoreau's light burns brightly within their souls. Their devotion to helping us experience the loving spiritual presence within each other is a testament to Thoreau's impact upon humanity. Martin Luther King had a famous dream about humanity's spiritual destiny—a dream that one day we would recognize all people as our brothers and sisters. I feel that Thoreau also had a dream, a dream that humanity would one day awaken to its true spiritual potential and begin to *live deliberately*. Perhaps, that day has come.

Thoreau: Perspectives from Others

Emerson to a young Thoreau: "Be an opener of doors for such as come after you."

By speaking as concretely as he does about his own historical situation, Thoreau expresses exactly that which is valid for all human history.

Martin Buber, Essay: "Man's Duty as Man"

It goes without saying that the teachings of Thoreau are alive today, indeed, they are more alive than ever before...As a result of his writings and personal witness, we are heirs to a legacy of creative protest.

Martin Luther King, Jr., *A Legacy of Creative Protest*

Thoreau inspires attitudes and offers strategies by which the individual, whatever his position, may at once more fully realize his dignity and potentiality as a human being.

John H. Hicks, *Thoreau in Our Season*

Thoreau died during the Civil War, but the ripples of influence spreading from his positive and self–contained personality are still expanding...To think that Thoreau has been made irrelevant by the Machine Age is to lose sight not merely of the point of his criticism, but of his actual historical position.

Lewis Mumford, *The Brown Decades*

Thoreau lived when men were appraising trees in terms of board feet, not in terms of watershed protection. His protests against that narrow outlook were among the first heard on this continent.

Former Supreme Court Justice William O. Douglas

In Thoreau's declaration of independence from the modern pace is where I find justification for my own propensities.

Robert Frost

Thoreau was not a penurious fanatic, who sought to practice bare living merely as a moral exercise: he wanted to obey Emerson's dictum to save on the lows levels and spend on the high ones. It is this that distinguishes him from the tedious people whose whole existence is absorbed in the practice of living on beans; simplification in Thoreau did not lead to the cult of simplicity: it led to a higher civilization.

Lewis Mumford, *Interpretations and Forecasts*

Walden is the handbook of an economy that endeavors to refute Adam Smith and transform the round of daily life into something noble.

Vernon Parrington, *Main Currents in American Thought*

Recent history and the present time have produced campaigners for justice of Thoreau's caliber. Many have been profoundly influenced by his writings and can attribute their success in part to his compelling and inspiring lead. Gandhi and Martin Luther King belong to this company, men who have sacrificed comfort and material advancement to win recognition fro the rights of their fellow human beings.

Rev. T.N.W. Bush, "Thoreau in South Africa"

Thoreau's "Civil Disobedience" stood for me, and for my leader in the Danish resistance movement, as a shining light with which we could examine the policy of complete passivity which our government had ordered for the whole Danish population (during the German occupation from 1940 to 1945). I lent Thoreau's books to friends, told them about him, and our circle grew.

Thoreau and the Danish Resistance
An Anonymous Memoir

Like Thoreau, I found my conscience coming into conflict with state authority. In 1954, at the height of the McCarthy hysteria, the State Legislature of New Hampshire authorized an inquiry for the avowed purpose of disclosing activities threatening the overthrow by force or violence of the government. As executive director of the World Fellowship Center, I was among those summoned to the inquiry...I was able to emerge victorious because I stood firm [in resisting their invasion of privacy because] studying Thoreau, I learned anew the great lesson of the Declaration of Independence that authority must be resisted if its demands violate conscience.

Willard Uphaus, Essay: "Conscience and Disobedience"

His words and attitude always suppose a better state of things than other men are acquainted with, and he will be the last man to be disappointed as the ages revolve.

Bronson Alcott

Emerson said it best when he summed up Thoreau's education, and thinking of the usual academic degree, conferred instead on his best friend that of the "bachelor of thought and nature."

Robert Richardson, *Henry Thoreau, A Life of the Mind*

Thoreau, more than anyone else in America, gave expression to a positive philosophy. His Walden, his Life on the Concord, his Cape Cod, to say nothing of his journals, were both directly and indirectly the starting point of a whole movement.

Lewis Mumford, *The Brown Decades*

On a typical page he may echo a Biblical phrase, quote from a metaphysical poet, translate a few words from an ancient classic, make an allusion to a Greek god, cite an authority on early American History, and toss in a metaphor from a Hindu text.

Walter Harding, *Thoreau in Our Season*

Walden is a profoundly rhetorical book, emerging unmistakably from the long New England preaching tradition; though here the trumpet call announces the best imaginable news rather than sounding apocalyptic warnings.

R.W.B. Lewis, *The American Adam*

The simple life, by whose gauge Henry Thoreau measured men and economies, aims at the most complete realization of the perfectibility innate in every person…He left behind a critique of our society and intimations of an undiminishable ideal to be fought for.

Leo Stoller, Essay: "Thoreau's Doctrine of Simplicity"

I will arise and go now, and go to Innisfree,
And a small cabin build there, of clay and wattles made:
Nine bean rows will I have there, a hive for the honeybee,
And live alone in the bee–loud glade.

William Butler Yeats, from
"The Lake Isle of Innisfree"

He loved Nature so well, was so happy in her solitude, that he became very jealous of cities and the sad work which their refinements and artifices made with man and his dwelling. The axe was always destroying his forest. "Thank God," he said, "they cannot cut down the clouds!"

Ralph Waldo Emerson, Essay: "Thoreau"

Thoreau's Intuitions of Our Contemporary Needs

Our life should be so active and progressive as to be a journey.

Journal, January 28, 1852

I know of no more encouraging fact than the unquestionable ability of man to elevate his life by a conscious endeavor.

Walden

The mass of men lead lives of quiet desperation...From the desperate city you go into the desperate country...A stereotyped but unconscious despair is concealed even under what are called the games and amusements of mankind.

Walden

There is an incessant influx of novelty into the world, yet we tolerate incredible dullness.

Walden

No method nor discipline can supersede the necessity of being forever on the alert.

Walden

Routine, conventionality, etc., etc. — how insensibly an undue attention to these things dissipates and impoverishes to the mind, robs it of its simplicity and strength.

Journal, July 7, 1851

We need pray for no higher heaven than what the pure senses can furnish, a purely sensuous life. Our present senses are rudiments of what they are destined to become.

A Week on the Concord and Merrimack Rivers

I would not have anyone adopt *my* mode of living on any account; for, beside that before he has fairly learned it, I may have found another for myself. I desire that there be as many different persons in the world as possible; but I would have each one be very careful to find out and pursue his own way, and not his father's or his mother's, or his neighbor's.

Walden

Again and again I am surprised to observe what an interval there is in what is called civilized life between the shell and the inhabitant of the shell—what a disproportion there is between the life of man and his conveniences and luxuries.

Journal, September 16, 1859

Men have come to such a pass that they frequently starve, not for want of necessities, but for want of luxuries.

Walden

We do not commonly live our full life—we live but a fraction of our life. Why do we not let on the flood, raise the gates, and set all the wheels in motion? He that hath ears to hear, let him hear. Employ your senses!

Journal, June 15, 1851

I would not forget that I deal with infinite and divine qualities in my fellow man. All men, indeed, are divine in their core of light.

Journal, August 15, 1845

It is by obeying the suggestions of a higher light within you that you escape from yourself, and in the transit, see with the unworn side of your eyes, travel totally new paths.

Journal, August 30, 1856

If a man does not keep pace with his companions, perhaps it is because he hears a different drummer. Let him step to the music which he hears, however measured or far away.

Walden

If an injustice is part of the necessary friction of the machine of government, let it go, let it go; perchance it will wear smooth—certainly the machine will wear out...but if it is of such a nature that it requires you to be the agent of its injustice to another, then I say, break the law. Let your life be a counter–friction to stop the machine.

Essay: "Civil Disobedience"

Woe to the generation that lets any higher faculty in its midst go unemployed!

Journal, December 22, 1853

THOREAU ON HIMSELF

"It is out of the shadow of my toil that I look
into the light."

Journals

Henry Thoreau's life remains a puzzle to some people
today, largely because he reveals both an optimistic and
pessimistic view of his life's mission. At times he delights in
his encounters with his contemporaries and seems to enjoy
their company. On other occasions, he seems disgusted with
both his own reality and the social realities around him.
Given this skepticism about himself in particular, and human
affairs in general, complete absorption in Nature became an
attractive option for him. Walden Pond, for example, could
become an extended metaphor describing his secret intuitions
about the soul. Thoreau could trust Nature, even if he could
not always trust himself or his contemporaries.

Rather than describing the basic themes in Thoreau's
life, I grant you the opportunity to explore Thoreau's life—
from his perspective—through selections from his writings.
As you read the selections that follow, refer to the
chronological chart beginning on page four to establish
correlation between events in his life and his writings. You
may want to record your initial impressions about Thoreau
before investigating other chapters in this book. Once you
have completed the book, re–evaluate your initial impressions to determine if any new insights have arisen. Do
not be discouraged if Thoreau remains somewhat ineffable,
for he even escapes being pinned down by the "experts," a
characteristic he shares with many other great minds such as
da Vinci, Einstein, Socrates, O'Keeffe, Jung, and Mozart.

Selections from Thoreau's *Journals*

March 21, 1840: I am freer than any planet....I can move away from public opinion, from government, from religion, from education, from society.

June 23, 1840: I cannot see the bottom of the sky, because I cannot see to the bottom of myself. It is the symbol of my own infinity.

February 3, 1841: My life must seem as if it were passing at a higher level than that which I occupy. It must possess a dignity which will not allow me to be familiar.

February 8, 1841: My journal is that of me which would else spill over and run to waste, gleanings from the field which in action I reap.

February 18, 1841: Sometimes I find that I have frequented a higher society during sleep, and my thoughts and actions proceed on a higher level in the morning.

February 26, 1841: What I am I am. *Being* is the great explainer.

February 26, 1841: Though I write everyday, yet when I say a good thing it seems as if I wrote but rarely.

February 27, 1841: My future deeds bestir themselves within me and move grandly towards a consummation, as ships go down the Thames. A steady onward motion I feel in me, as still as that, or like some vast, snowy cloud, whose shadow first is seen across the fields.

August 9, 1841: If I am not I, who will be?

March 30, 1841: I find my life grown slovenly when it does not exercise a constant supervision over itself. Its deeds accumulate.

April 7, 1841: My life will wait for nobody, but is being matured still irresistibly while I go about the streets...It will cut its own channel like the mountain stream, which by the longest ridges and by level prairies is not kept from the sea finally.

August 28, 1841: My life hath been the poem I
                         would have writ,
                    But I could not live and
                         live to utter it.

September 2, 1841: When I write verses I serve my thoughts as I do tumblers; I rap them to see if they sing.

November 30, 1841: My eyes look inward, not without,
                         And I but hear myself,
                         And this new wealth which I have got
                         Is part of my own pelf.

March 11, 1842: I must not be for myself, but God's work and that is always good.

March 11, 1842: Why, God, did you include me in your great scheme?

March 11, 1842: I feel as if I could at any time resign my life and the responsibility of living into God's hands, and become as innocent and free from care as a plant or stone.

March 23, 1842: I never compass my own ends. God schemes for me.

April 3, 1842: I cannot convince myself. God must convince. I can calculate a problem in arithmetic, but not in morality.

July 6, 1845: Life, who knows what it is, what it does? If I am not quite right here, I am less wrong than before. (This was his third day at Walden Pond.)

August 23, 1845: I find an instinct in me conducting to a mystic spiritual life, and also another to a primitive savage life.

July 16, 1850: All I can say is that I live and breath and have my thoughts.

July 16, 1850: From time to time I overlook the promised land; the moment I begin to look there, men and institutions get out of the way that I may see.

July 16, 1850: As to conforming outwardly, and living you own life inwardly, I have not a very high opinion of that.

November 16, 1850: My Journal should be the record of my lore. I would write in it only of the things that I love, my affection for any aspect of the world, what I love to think of.

November 16, 1850: I feel ripe for something, yet do nothing, can't discover what that thing is. I feel fertile; it is seed time within me.

November 23, 1850: I find it to be the height of wisdom not to endeavor to oversee myself and live a life of prudence and common sense, but to see over and above myself, entertain sublime conjectures, to make myself the thoroughfare of thrilling thoughts, live all that can be lived.

November 25, 1850: I feel a little alarmed when it happens that I have walked a mile into the woods bodily, without getting there in spirit....What business have I in the woods, if I am thinking of something out of the woods?

1851: I would feign keep a journal which should contain those thoughts and impressions which I am most liable to forget that I have had.

July 16, 1851: Let me forever go in search of myself; never for a moment think that I have found myself; be as a stranger to myself, never a familiar.

July 16, 1851: As I regard myself, so I am.

August 7, 1851: How to extract honey from the flower of the world. That is my every–day business. I am as busy as a bee about it.

February 5, 1852: Time never passes so rapidly and unaccountably as when I am engaged in recording my thoughts.

March 5, 1853: The fact is I am a mystic, a transcendentalist, and a natural philosopher to boot.

August 18, 1856: My profession is writing...I know that no subject is trivial for me, tried by ordinary standards.

October 26, 1857: My loftiest thought is somewhat like an eagle that suddenly comes into the field of view, suggesting great things and thrilling the beholder.

August 27, 1859: I served my apprenticeship and have since done some considerable journey–work in the huckleberry field...It was itself some of the best schooling I got.

April 1, 1860: I am surprised that my affirmations or utterances come to me ready–made—not forethought,— so that I occasionally awake in the night simply to let fall ripe a statement which I had never consciously considered before.

Walden period journal fragments: My intercourse with men is governed by the same laws as my intercourse with nature./ It has not been my design to live cheaply, but only to live as I could, not devoting much time to getting a living. I made the most of what means were already got.

Selections from *Walden*

I do not propose to write an ode to dejection, but to brag as lustily as chanticleer in the morning, standing on his roost, if only to wake my neighbors up.

I went to the woods because I wished to live deliberately, to front only the essential facts of life, and see if I could learn what I had to teach, and not, when it came time to die, discover that I had not lived.

If I seem to boast more than is becoming, my excuse is that I brag for humanity rather than for myself.

I would observe, by the way, that it costs me nothing for curtains, for I have no gazers to shut out but the sun and moon, and I am willing that they should look in.

Time is but the stream I go a–fishing in.

I am convinced, both by faith and experience, that to maintain one's self on this earth is not a hardship, but a pastime, if we will live simply and wisely. It is not necessary that a man should earn his living by the sweat of his brow, unless he sweats easier than I do.

I have always been regretting that I was not as wise as the day I was born. The intellect is a cleaver; it discerns and rifts its way into the secret of things.

I had this advantage, at least, over those who were obliged to look abroad for amusement, to society and the theatre, that my life itself was my amusement and it never ceased to be novel.

Some of my pleasantest hours were during the long rainstorms in spring or fall, which confined me to the house for the afternoon as well as the forenoon, soothed by their ceaseless roar and pelting; when an early twilight in a long evening in which many thoughts had time to take root and unfold themselves.

I am no more lonely than a single mullein or dandelion in a pasture, or a bean leaf, or a horse–fly, or a bumble–bee. I am no more lonely than the Mill Brook, or a weathercock, or the northstar, or a south wind, or a January thaw, or the first spider in a new house.

Rather than love, than money, than fame, give me truth.
I prefer the natural sky to an opium–eater's heaven.

I had three chairs in my house; one for solitude, two for friendship, three for society.

In warm evenings, I frequently sat in the boat playing the flute, and saw the perch, which I seemed to have charmed, hovering around me.

As I stand over the insect crawling amid the pine needles on the forest floor, and endeavoring to conceal itself from my sight, and hide its head from me who might be its benefactor, I am reminded of the greater Benefactor and Intelligence that stands over me, the human insect.

I am convinced that if all men lived as simply as I did, thieving and robbery would be unknown.

However intense the experience, I am conscious of the presence and criticism of a part of me, which, as it were, is not a part of me, but a spectator, sharing no experience, but taking note of it.

I left the woods for as good a reason as I went there. Perhaps it seemed to me that I had several more lives to live, and I could not spare any more time for that one.

I have learned this, at least, by my experiment; that if one advances confidently in the direction of his dreams and endeavors to the life which he has imagined, he will meet with success unexpected in common hours.

Selections from Thoreau's other Writings

I hear beyond the range of sound
I see beyond the range of sight
New earths and skies and seas around
And in my day the sun doth pale his light.

Poem, "Inspiration"

To set about living a true life is to go on a journey to a
distant country, gradually to find ourselves surrounded by
new scenes and new men; and as long as the old are around
me, I know that I am not in any true sense living a new or
better life.

Letter to Harrison Blake, March 27, 1848

I feel addressed and probed even to the remotest parts of my
being when one nobly shows, even in trivial things, an
implicit faith in me.

Letter to Ralph W. Emerson, February 12, 1843

There is in my nature, methinks, a singular yearning toward
all wildness.

Sunday: A Week on the Concord and Merrimack Rivers

The only obligation which I have a right to assume is to do at
any time what I think right.

I was not born to be forced. I will breathe after my own
fashion. They only can force me who obey a higher law than
I.

I do not wish to quarrel with any man or nation. I do not
wish to split hairs, or set myself up as better than my
neighbors.

It is not many moments that I live under a government, even
in this world.

I please myself with imagining a State which at least can
afford to be just to all men, and to treat the individual with
respect as a neighbor; which even would not think it
inconsistent with its own repose if a few were to live aloof

from it, not meddling with it, nor embraced by it…A State which bore this kind of fruit, and suffered it to drop off as fast as it ripened, would prepare the way for a still more perfect and glorious State, which also I have imagined, but not yet anywhere seen.

Selections above are from "Civil Disobedience"

I trust that you will pardon me for being here. I do not wish to force my thoughts upon you, but I feel forced myself.

Opening from address before Concord town meeting:
"A Plea for Captain John Brown"

TRUE FRIENDSHIP:
Emerson on Thoreau &
Thoreau on Emerson

Several prominent factors united early in Thoreau's life which helped secure his place in history. His intimate, sometimes intense, friendship with his mentor Ralph Waldo Emerson was, perhaps, the most significant contribution to his development as a writer, thinker, and student of Nature. Emerson's influence upon Thoreau actually began as the young Harvard student read Emerson's provocative book, *Nature*, and was intrigued by the refreshing ideas he encountered. After graduating from Harvard in 1837, Thoreau returned to his native Concord to meet with the person responsible for such stimulating ideas about Nature and our relationship with it.

At the time of their meeting, Emerson was thirty–four, while Thoreau was twenty. Emerson was enough older to be an effective mentor, yet still close enough in age to Thoreau through his passion for life and his stimulating circle of friends for Thoreau to feel a strong affinity for his older friend. Their friendship grew swiftly, and Emerson spent considerable energy helping Thoreau develop the extraordinary creative potential he intuited to be present in his younger companion. Almost immediately, Emerson invited Thoreau to attend meetings and discussions with other prominent thinkers and writers who lived in Concord. He included Thoreau in his efforts to launch the Transcendentalist journal, *The Dial*. Thoreau responded to his friend's encouragement with great enthusiasm and felt inspired by the confidence Emerson had placed in him.

As their friendship matured, Thoreau moved into Emerson's home. At times he occupied a room within the household, and at other times he lived in a small shed behind the barn. Emerson even provided the parcel of land upon which Thoreau built his cabin by Walden Pond during his experiment in living deliberately. Thoreau repaid Emerson by performing chores around the house. He even became the surrogate father for the young children when Emerson visited Europe or embarked on speaking tours. Their relationship, although occasionally intense and stormy, exhibited the spiritual bonds found in true friendships.

Emerson's essay "Friendship" reflects his friendship with Thoreau. Emerson presents many factors that contribute to such a relationship, as well as the benefits of having such a relationship. He then synthesizes these ideas into two essential requirements for true friendship. They are:

1) TRUTH — friends must avoid deception and dishonesty with each other, even when it would be more comfortable for both people if a deception had been created

2) TENDERNESS — friends must not only be honest and truthful with one another, but they also must share their emotional sensitivities with each other; friends must be genuine human beings in the truest sense of the term

Friendship is life itself

Emerson's essay portrayed friendship to be more than simple caring and respect for another person, more than just enjoying another person's company, or even more than having feelings of affection for another person. *Friendship is life itself*, life expressed in its richest, most fully realized dimension. A true friend is someone with whom you can discard your rationalizations and pretenses so that you can develop your unique human potential without fear. A true friend is someone whose soul joins with yours in exploration of the universe and with whom you rejoice in your discoveries. Thoreau found in this essay not only a description of his friendship with Emerson, but also the archetypal friendship described throughout human history such as the friendship between Socrates and Plato or Damon and Pythias.

Undoubtedly, Thoreau's ideas about friendship were influenced by these and other legendary friendships. These epic testaments to friendship contributed to his understanding of his relationship with Emerson. Socrates, the older mentor, and Plato, the younger disciple, exemplified in many way his friendship with Emerson. Socrates' penetrating, often relentless, questions about "Truth" provoked Plato to develop his own ideas on the subject into one of humanity's most eloquent expressions of Truth. Yet, in spite of Socrates' often intense provocation, Plato remained tenaciously loyal to his mentor, even when such fidelity could have exposed him to accusations similar to those facing Socrates. Damon and Pythias' story also presents loyalty and compassion to be essential components of friendship. Even at the risk of his own life, Damon could not tolerate living with the thought that he had failed to do everything possible to secure the release of his friend. Damon realized that, without an intimate friendship with Pythias, his own life would lose some of its value.

Thoreau, perhaps as a young man intuiting his place in history, began to draw upon his knowledge of these classic friendships and upon his current experiences with Emerson to formulate his own ideas about friendship and the role that it plays in our development. Likewise, Emerson grew from his intimate and highly spirited relationship with Thoreau. The following selections from their writings reveal these influences. Their ideas, if we are open to them, can enhance our own understanding of friendship and the role that it plays in attaining our highest mental and spiritual potential.

EMERSON ON THOREAU

Selections from Emerson's Essay, "Thoreau"

There was an excellent wisdom in him, proper to a rare class of men, which showed him the material world as a means and symbol.

He lived for the day, not encumbered and mortified by his memory.

His power of observation seemed to indicate additional senses. He saw as with a microscope, heard with a hearing aid, and his memory was a photographic register of all he saw and heard.

Thoreau was sincerity itself, and he might fortify the convictions of the prophets in the ethical laws by his holy living....He was a speaker and actor of truth.

To him there was no such thing as size. The pond was a small ocean; the Atlantic a large Walden.

His study of Nature was a perpetual ornament to him, and it inspired his friends with curiosity to see the world through his eyes.

His interest in the flower or the bird lay very deep in his mind; it was connected with Nature, and the meaning of Nature was never attempted to be defined by him.

In his youth he said, 'The other world is all my art; my pencils will draw no other.' This was the muse and genius that ruled his opinions, conversation, studies, work, and course of life.

He knew how to sit immovable, a part of the rock he rested upon, until the bird, the reptile, the fish, which had retired away from him should come back and resume its habits, nay, moved by curiosity, should come to him and watch him.

Thoreau chose to be rich by making his wants few and supplying them himself.

Hermit and stoic as he was, he was really fond of sympathy, and threw himself heartily and childlike into the company of young people whom he loved.

Not a particle of respect had he to the opinions of any man or body of men, but homage solely to the truth itself.

Selections from Emerson's *Journals*

In reading [Thoreau's *Journals*] him, I find the same thought, the same spirit that is in me, but he takes it a step beyond, and illustrates by excellent images that which I would have conveyed in a sleepy generality.

Mr. Webster told Congress how much the war cost, but voted for the war and sends his son to it....My friend Mr. Thoreau has gone to jail rather than pay his tax.

Thoreau gives me, in flesh and blood, my own ethics. He is far more real, and daily obeying them, than I.

Henry Thoreau remains erect, calm, self subsistent, before me and, I read him not only truly in his Journal, but he is not long out of mind when I talk, and, as today, row from the pond. He chose wisely to be the bachelor of thought and nature that he was—how near to the old monks in their ascetic religion! [Journal entry three weeks after Thoreau's death]

My good Henry Thoreau made this else solitary afternoon sunny with his simplicity and clean perception...We agreed that seeing the stars through a telescope would be worth all the astronomy lectures in the world.

Thoreau. Perhaps his fancy for Walt Whitman grew out of his taste for wild nature, for an otter, a woodchuck, or a loon.

Thoreau wants a fallacy to expose, a blunder to pillory, requires a sense of victory, a roll of the drums, to call his powers into full exercise.

Last night came to me a beautiful poem from Henry Thoreau, "Sympathy." The purest strain, and the loftiest, I think that has yet pealed from this American forest.

Yesterday to the Sawmill Brook with Thoreau. He was in search of yellow violets. He thinks he could tell by the flowers what day of the month it is, within two days.
Last night Henry Thoreau read me verses which pleased, if not by the beauty of particular lines, yet by the honest truth, and by the length of flight and the strength of wing; for most of our poets are only writers of lines or of epigrams.

It seemed as if the breezes brought him,
It seemed as if the sparrows taught him.

Lines from Emerson's poem, "Woodnotes about Thoreau"

From Emerson's Eulogy at Thoreau's Funeral

"The country knows not yet, or in the least part, how great a son it has lost. It seems an injury that he should leave in the midst his broken task which none else can finish, a kind of indignity to so noble a soul that he should depart out of Nature before he has really been shown to his peers for what he is. But he, at least, is content. His soul was made for the noblest society; he had in a short life exhausted the capabilities of this world; wherever there is knowledge, wherever there is virtue, wherever there is beauty, he will find a home."

As Emerson turned to walk away from the freshly covered grave, he exclaimed: "He had a beautiful soul, he had a beautiful soul."

THOREAU ON EMERSON AND FRIENDSHIP

Thoreau's first journal entry [October 22, 1837], prompted by Emerson's insistence that he keep one: "What are you doing now?" he asked. "Do you keep a journal?" So I make my first entry today.

The most I can do for my friend is simply to be his friend....If he knows that I am happy in loving him, he will want no other reward. Is not friendship divine in this?

Journals, February 7, 1841

The world has never learned what men can build each other up to be—when both master and pupil work in love.

Letter to Emerson, February, 1841

Our friend must be broad. His must be an atmosphere co-extensive with the universe, in which we can expand and breathe.

Journals, November 24, 1850

We must accept or refuse one another as we are. I could tame a hyena more easily than my Friend. He is a material no tool of mine will work.

A Week on the Concord and Merrimack Rivers

Friends are those who feel their interests to be one. Each knows that the other might as well have said what he said.

Journals, March 20, 1842

To attain a true relation to one human being is enough to make a year memorable.

Journals, March 30, 1851

Emerson is a critic, poet, philosopher and lives a far more intense life; seeks to realize a divine life; his affections and intellect equally developed. He has advanced further, and a new heaven opens to him...More of the divine is realized in him than in any other.

Journals, 1845

To his Friend a man's peculiar character appears in every feature and in every action, and it is thus drawn out and improved by him.

A Week...

We inspire friendship in men when we have contracted friendship with the gods.

Journals, June 9, 1850

Some men may be acquaintances merely, but one whom I have been accustomed to regard, to idealize, to have dreams about as a friend, and mix up intimately with myself, can never denigrate into an acquaintance.

Journals, November 24, 1850

Emerson has special talents unequaled. The divine in man has no more easy, methodically distinct expression. His personal influence upon young persons is greater than any man's. In his world every man would be a poet. Love would reign, Beauty would take place, Man and Nature would harmonize.

Journals, 1845–47

My friend is not of some other race or family of men, but flesh of my flesh, bone of my bone. He is my brother.

A Week...

Of our friends we do not complain to others; we would not disturb the foundations of confidence.

Journals, February 15, 1851

Emerson does not consider things in respect to their essential utility, but in an important partial and relative way, as works of art.

Journals, 1845–47

Friends will not only live in harmony, but in melody.

Journals, April 30, 1841

In company, that person who alone can understand you, you cannot get out of your mind is your friend.

Journals, March 25, 1842

In friendship, we worship moral beauty without the formality of religion.

Journals, 1837-47

The friend asks no return but that his friend will religiously accept and wear, and not disgrace, his apotheosis of him. They will cherish each other's hopes. They are kind to each other's dreams.

A Week...

When I observe my friend's conduct towards others, then chiefly I learn the traits in his character.

Journals, February 6, 1841

Sometimes we are said to love another, that is, to stand in a true relation to our friend, so that we give the best to, and receive the best from, him. Between whom there is hearty truth, there is love, and in proportion to our truthfulness and confidence in one another, our lives are divine and miraculous, and answer to our ideal.

A Week...

Friends are the ancient and honorable of the earth; the oldest men did not begin friendship. It is older than Hindostan and the Chinese Empire....There is a friendliness between the sun and the earth in pleasant weather.

Journals, April 8, 1841

The death of friends should inspire us as much as their lives.

Journals, February 2, 1842

True friendship is so firm a league that its maintenance falls into the even tenor of our lives, and is no tie, but is the continuance of our life's thread.

Journals, April 11, 1841

I care not for the man who would make the highest use of me short of an all–adventuring friendship.

Journals, March 25, 1842

A friend is one who incessantly pays us the compliment of expecting from us all the virtues, and who can appreciate them in us.

A Week...

THOREAU ON HUMANITY

"Speak to men as to gods and you will not be insincere."

Journals, May 9, 1841

"Men will lie on their backs talking about the fall of men, and never make an effort to get up."

Life Without Principle

Looking at these two quotations, it might be hard to determine if Thoreau is an idealist or a realist concerning human nature. Are we the divine beings worthy of great respect presented in the first quotation? Or, is our true nature that of the apathetic, disconsolate creature worthy only of pity in the second quotation? This enigma, perhaps more than any other Thoreau encountered, created considerable deliberation and speculation. Certainly Emerson's belief in humanity's divine nature and our unlimited capacity to activate our spiritual potential affected Thoreau's own thinking on the subject. Thoreau did agree *in principle* with his friend; however, his penetrating observations of humanity *in action* generated significant skepticism about our true nature. It was not until he wrote of his experiments in practical spirituality at Walden Pond that we discover how he resolved the issue.

Thoreau, even before his two years at Walden, was an incessantly mindful spectator of the human drama. He often wondered how we could possess such tremendous spiritual potential and yet so often behave like spoiled, self–centered brats. Others such as Confucius, Carlyle, and Kant also had speculated about the discrepancy between our true potential and our actualization of that potential. Thoreau, however, went far beyond speculation on the matter. The Walden Pond experience provided sufficient distance between himself and society for him to render a conclusion about human nature that future leaders such as Gandhi and Martin Luther King would acknowledge as having influenced their own thinking.

In the solitude of Walden Pond, Thoreau contemplated humanity in action and discovered that we essentially have two separate natures: spiritual and animal/instinctual. Thoreau's intimate relationship with Nature, and his many thought–provoking discussions with Emerson, already had helped him recognize the divine spirit that permeates Nature, humanity included. His journals reveal a deep joy and exuberance at the discovery of humanity's "divine core of light" as a distinct and accessible entity within us. Emerson's guidance helped him become reliant upon this divine inner core, and Thoreau's experience at Walden nurtured and expanded his own spiritual dimension. While at Walden, he realized that humanity's spiritual core could assist us in reaching our highest potential; however, as he surveyed humanity in action, he found very few people developing a spiritual life. This led him to explore the other component of our nature, the animal/instinctual, as a possible reason for the discrepancy.

Our animal/instinctual nature is the "person" within us whose characteristics include instinctual behaviors such as territorially, mating, food–gathering, self–defense, and other self–preserving/self–serving activities. The animal portion of human nature perceives a "me against the world" or "survival of the fittest" reality. Even the more "civilized" animal in modern society behaves instinctually as if it were in a desperate survival contest with other elements of creation. A human's animal nature, because its primary focus is limited to self–preservation activities, does not experience its spiritual unity with the Transcendent or with Nature.

The instinctual side of humanity, as Thoreau realized from his observations in Nature, was a vestige from our early, pre–civilized days on the planet; yet, it somehow still affected our behavior, even in the most civilized societies. One explanation for the animalistic domination of our spiritual nature lies in the materialist-oriented philosophical, religious, and scientific mindset prevalent in the West since Francis Bacon had split spirit and Nature in the early seventeenth century. Bacon's emphasis upon the material or natural side of creation, and his cynicism regarding the spiritual, diminished awareness of our spiritual nature. In addition, Adam Smith's doctrine of "enlightened self–interest" which proclaimed that our animalistic self-serving actions were somehow to be championed as our salvation further enlarged the rift between our spiritual and material natures. Smith's ideas maintained that it was both *necessary* and *desirable* for us to compete aggressively with each other when it came to human interactions, so that we could enjoy material prosperity. Survival of the fittest in a materialistic world became humanity's *modus operandi*.

Thoreau realized while living deliberately at Walden Pond that, if we are to attain our highest potential, our spiritual nature must transform our animalistic, materialistic nature into a new orientation towards the universe. In the chapter "Higher Laws," he writes that even though our animal nature awakens in proportion as our spiritual nature slumbers, "the spirit can pervade and control every member and function of the body, and transmute the grossest sensuality into purity and devotion." He continues:

> Man at once flows to God when the channel
> of purity is open....He is blessed who is
> assured that the animal is dying out in him
> day by day, and the divine being established.

Thoreau now seems to understand human nature in a more comprehensive manner than seeing us through the eyes of either a realist or an idealist. He understands that we are beings whose spiritual nature slumbers because our animal nature remains virile and active, fighting against the natural world in a desperate struggle to survive. In modern times, we no longer face the hostility of the jungle or desert in order to survive; instead, we face the hostility of a materialistic society whose various media bombard us with the message essential to their survival: "living well is the best revenge."

To the extent that humanity continues to sleepwalk in our animalistic stupor, we will continue in our quest for dominion over Nature and over each other. On the other hand, to the extent that we awaken our higher spiritual nature and let it guide us, the animal will slumber. We then can establish a divine purpose for our lives. Human nature, from this perspective, makes our lives out to be a great challenge. Thoreau maintains that it is our response to this challenge that gives meaning to life.

Men have become the tools of their tools.

Journals, 1845

The more we know about the ancients, the more we know about the moderns.

Journals, September 2, 1851

It is remarkable how long men will believe in the bottomless of a pond without taking the trouble to sound it.

Walden

Why level downward to our dullest perception always, and praise that as common sense? The commonest sense is the sense of men asleep.

Walden

Man is like a cork which no tempest can sink, but it will float securely to its haven at last.

Journals, January 16 1838

Why should we be in such desperate haste to succeed and in such desperate enterprises?

Walden

Society is commonly too cheap. We meet at very short intervals, not having had time to acquire any new value for each other.

Walden

With a little more deliberation in the choice of their pursuits, all men would perhaps become essentially students and observers, for their nature and destiny are interesting to all alike.

Walden

The words of some men are thrown forcibly against you and adhere like burrs.

Journals, June 4, 1838

Man has a million eyes, and the race knows infinitely more than the individual. Consent to be wise through your race.

Journals, September, 1850

The youth gets materials together to build a bridge to the moon, or perchance a palace or temple on the earth, and at length, the middle–aged man concludes to build a woodshed with them.

Journals, July, 14, 1857

Most men, even in this comparatively free country, through mere ignorance and mistake, are so preoccupied with the factitious cares and superfluously coarse labors of life that its finer fruits cannot be plucked by them.

Walden

Thank God, men cannot as yet fly, and lay waste to the sky as well as to the earth.

Journals, January 3, 1861

The man of character never gets a holiday. Our true character silently underlies all our words and actions as the granite underlies the other strata.

Journals, May 3, 1841

Men do not after all meet on the ground of their real acquaintance and actual understanding of one another, but degrade themselves immediately into the puppets of convention.

Journals, March 30, 1842

I am wont to think that men are not so much the keepers of herds, as herds are the keepers of men.

Walden

Character is genius settled. It can maintain itself against the world, and if it relapses, it repents.

Journals, March 2, 1842

Man is the artifice of his own happiness. Let him beware
how he complains of the disposition of circumstances, for it
is his own disposition he blames.

Journals, January 21, 1838

Of all phenomena, my own race is the most mysterious and
undiscoverable.

Journals, June 29, 1840

THOREAU ON NATURE

"This earth which is spread out like a map around me is but the lining of my inmost soul exposed."

Journals, May 23, 1854

The concept of Nature as a spiritual entity underlies human religious experience from Ice Age cave art depicting the Goddess/Mother Earth to such spiritual practices as Taoism, Paganism, Shamanism, and Christian Mysticism. Humanity intuitively knows that Nature existed long before our emergence upon the planet, both as a species and as an individual member of the species. We also realize that Nature will endure long after our individual deaths. Sensing that Nature has "power" over life and death, our religious quests have searched for the source of Nature's powers and have found it to be God, the Goddess, the Great Spirit, Nzambi Mpungu, the Tao, *et al.*

Virtually all religions acknowledge, as does Thoreau in the quotation above, that Nature and our soul have an intimate relationship with each other. Both Nature and our souls are "created" by the Universal Creative Essence, they contain both physical and spiritual realities, and they are subject to temporal laws, yet also exist apart from time. The primary exception to acknowledging the spiritual kinship between ourselves and Nature is historic Christianity, Thoreau's childhood religion. As a child, Thoreau learned that Nature was "sinful" and cast away from God. Nature, therefore, was nothing more than a dead, spiritually inert hulk from which humans were to carve out our consolation prize—*material possessions*—for being sinners. Humans had no escape from this fallen state other than to turn to the historic Jesus for salvation.

As a young man, Thoreau intuited that something was amiss in this religious perspective. His soul had sensed a kinship with Nature and her spiritual principles long before his mind had acquired an intellectual understanding of this kinship. Thoreau, as a Harvard student, read Emerson's provocative book, *Nature*, which was his first step in acquiring the knowledge that his soul already had intuited. Thoreau discovered one passage in particular which prompted him to reconsider what his childhood religious experiences had told him about Nature:

> The lover of nature is he whose inward and outward senses are still truly adjusted to each other; who has retained the spirit of infancy even into the era of manhood. His intercourse with heaven and earth becomes part of his daily food.

Thoreau now understood Nature to be an object of two different sets of sense organs, each with a different target and mode of operation. One set, our five "outer" senses, is focused upon Nature's physical reality (sights, smells, sounds, tastes, and touches). The other set, our inner, intuitive senses, is focused "within" us, upon our soul and its connections with Nature's Transcendental reality.

Having two sets of sense organs capable of experiencing Nature, however, presents a potential dilemma—a dilemma that Emerson and Thoreau solved by quite different means. Emerson, who keenly felt God's presence within us, believed that we should focus our attention upon our soul's intuitive faculties and use them as a starting point if we desire to transcend Nature's physical reality and discover her spiritual energies. His intercourse with Nature begins with a quiet, inner experience as a prerequisite for deriving benefit from the outer sensory experience. Emerson finds God within us who will reveal God all around us.

Thoreau, on the other hand, finds God all around us in Nature who will reveal the God within us. He felt that Nature is really just "us" in a slightly different dressing. That being the case, we should use our outer sense organs to transcend Nature's physical reality in order to discern her hidden spiritual energies. Thoreau starts at the outer level, transcends what he sees, hears, touches, etc. around him, and aligns his soul with the spiritual essence that he has discerned in Nature. You may be wondering: "What difference does it make if I start on the inner or outer level if both Emerson's and Thoreau's processes will lead me into a deeper spiritual relationship with Nature?" Perhaps you have guessed the primary difference.

Emerson's Method: Emerson, a student of Eastern contemplative methods, recognizes the inherent difficulty humanity has in approaching our inner world—most of have lost contact with our inner, spiritual reality. Emerson advocates we quiet the mind and call upon God's presence within us to guide us towards intimacy with Nature.

Thoreau's Method: Thoreau also recognizes the necessity of having a disciplined mind if we are to unite with Nature, but he feels that discipline begins when we focus our minds upon Nature and let her spiritual energies guide us. Our life's goal, according to Thoreau, is to re–ally ourselves with Nature, the source of our earthly existence. Once we experience our connection with Nature, then we will nurture our bonds with God, the Transcendent.

It is the marriage of our soul with Nature that makes the intellect fruitful, that gives birth to the imagination.

Journals, August 20, 1851

My profession is always to be alert, to find God in nature, to know God's lurking places, to attend all the oratorios and the operas in nature.

Letter to Ralph Waldo Emerson

Heaven is under our feet as well as over our heads.

Walden

Every part of nature teaches us that the passing away of one life is the making of room for another. The oak lies down to the ground, leaving within its rind a rich, virgin mould, which will impart a vigorous life to an infant forest.

Journals, October 24, 1837
[Thoreau's third day of keeping a journal]

Shall I not have intelligence with the earth? Am I not partly leaves and vegetable mould myself?

Walden

The revelations of nature are infinitely glorious and cheering, hinting to us of a remote future, of possibilities untold.

Journals, May 21, 1851

Nature will bear the closest inspection; she invites us to lay our eye level with the smallest leaf, and take an insect view of its plane. She has no interstices; every part is full of life.

A Natural History of Massachusetts

Nature, even when she is scant and thin outwardly, contents us still by the assurance of a certain generosity at the roots.

Journals, August 13, 1841

There is nothing so sanative, so poetic as a walk in the woods...Nothing so inspires me and excites serene and profitable thought.

Journals, January 7, 1857

I see, smell, taste, hear, feel that everlasting something to which we all are allied, at one with our maker.

A Week upon the Concord and Merrimack Rivers

How is it that man always feels like an interloper in nature, as if he had intruded on the domains of the bird and beast?

Journals, March 31, 1842

I think that the existence of man in nature is the divinest and startling of all facts. It is a fact which few have realized.

Journals, May 21, 1851

If we knew all the laws of Nature, we should need only one fact, or the description of one actual phenomenon, to infer all the particular results at that point. Now we know only a few laws, and our result is vitiated, not, of course, by any confusion or irregularity in Nature, but by our ignorance...Our notions of law and harmony are commonly confined to those instances which we detect; but the harmony which results from a far greater number of seemingly conflicting, but really concurring, laws which we have not detected is still more wonderful.

Walden

This stillness, solitude, wildness of nature is a kind of thorough wort or boneset to my intellect. This is what I go out to seek.

Journals, January 7, 1857

It is a luxury to muse by a wall–side in the sunshine of a September afternoon,—to cuddle down under a gray stone, and harken to the siren call of the cricket...I know of no word so fit to express this disposition of nature as *alma natura*.

Journals, September 20, 1838

There seems to be two sides to this world, presented to us at different times, as we see things in growth or dissolution, in life or death. For seen with the eye of a poet, as God sees them, all are beautiful; but seen with the eye of memory, they are dead and offensive.

Journals, March 13, 1842

On the outside all the life of the earth is expressed in the animal or vegetable, but make a deep cut in it and you find it vital; you find in it the very anticipation of the vegetable leaf or animal.

Journals, March 2, 1854

This is a delicious evening, when the whole body is one sense, and imbibes delight through every pore. I come and go with a strange liberty in Nature, a part of herself.

Walden

When I hear a robin sing at sunset, I cannot help contrasting the equanimity of nature with man's bustle and impatience.

Journals, April 4, 1841

There can be no very black melancholy to him who lives in the midst of Nature and has his senses still.

Walden

I would be glad if all the meadows on the earth were left in a wild state, if that were the consequence of men's beginning to redeem themselves.

Walden

I am like a bee searching the livelong day for the sweets of nature. Do I not impregnate and intermix the flowers, produce rare and finer varieties by transferring my eyes from one flower to another.

Journals, September 7, 1851

Nature has no human inhabitant who appreciates her. The birds with their plumage and their notes are in harmony with the flowers, but what youth or maiden conspires with the wild luxuriant beauty of Nature? She flourishes most alone, far from the towns where they reside. Talk of heaven! Ye disgrace earth.

Walden

The sudden revolutions of these times and this generation have acquired a very exaggerated importance. They do not interest me much, for they are not in harmony with the longer periods of nature.

Journals, January 7, 1842

I came to love my rows, my beans...they attached me to the earth.

Walden

Of thee, O earth, are my bone and sinew made; to thee, O sun, am I brother. To this dust my body will gladly return; I am of thee.

Journals, November 7, 1851

To him who contemplates a trait of natural beauty, no harm or disappointment can come. The doctrines of despair, of spiritual or political tyranny or servitude, were never taught by such as shared the serenity of nature.

Essay: "A Natural History of Massachusetts"

I think that I cannot preserve my health and spirits, unless I spend four hours a day at least—and it is commonly more than that—sauntering through the woods and over the hills and fields, absolutely free from all worldly engagements.

Essay: "Walking"

Probe the universe in a myriad of points...He is a wise man who has taken many views; to whom stones and plants and animals and a myriad of objects have each suggested something, contributed something.

Journals, September 4, 1851

We need the tonic of wildness—to wade sometimes in marshes where the bittern and the meadow hen lurk, to smell the whispering sedge where only some wilder and more solitary fowl builds her nest, and the mink crawls with its belly close to the ground.

Walden

My pulse must beat with Nature. After a hard day's work Let us spend one day as deliberately as Nature.

Walden

How important is a constant intercourse with nature and the contemplation of natural phenomena to the preservation of moral and intellectual health. The discipline of the schools or of business can never impart such serenity to the mind.

Journals, May 6, 1851

Music is the sound of the circulation in nature's veins. It is the flux which melts nature. Men dance to it, glasses ring and vibrate, and the fields seem to undulate. The healthy ear always hears it, nearer or remote.

Journals, April 24, 1841

To ears that have expanded, what a harp this world is!

Journals, July 21, 1851

PART TWO:
Experiments in Practical Spirituality

— Inspired by —

- ## Henry Thoreau
- ## Native Americans
- ## Ernest Holmes
- ## Carl Jung

"What I begin by reading, I must finish by acting."

Thoreau, *Journals,*

O Mother Earth, may the steps we take in life upon you be sacred.

Oglala Sioux Prayer for Mother Earth

"We should learn to control our thought processes and bring them into line with Reality."

Ernest Holmes, *The Science of Mind*

"The important thing is not to *know* the truth, but to *experience* it."

Carl Jung, *Collected Works*

The ideas above affirm that knowledge alone will not help us live deliberately. Thoreau, Native Americans, Holmes, and Jung—the primary resources for the following activities—realized that knowledge must guide our footsteps if we are to live deliberately. *Knowledge must inspire action.*

Sources of Inspiration for the Experiments

Thoreau felt most strongly that knowledge pursued for its own sake could become an impediment to our progress. To Thoreau, conducting practical experiments in living more deliberately was far more valuable in developing our highest potential than was a Faustian acquisition of the latest scientific or philosophical knowledge. His journals—and especially his *Walden*—offer invaluable assistance to contemporary audiences who seek to live more deliberately by applying spiritual principles in daily life.

Another stimulus for the following activities in applied spirituality is Native American wisdom and practices, because it is wisdom derived from life experiences. The Native American lifestyle is "living deliberately."

The writings of Ernest Holmes, founder of the Religious Science movement, are another source of inspiration for the activities. Holmes' book, *The Science of Mind*, is a treasure–trove of spiritual wisdom that we can apply in our daily lives. Holmes and other Religious Science/New Thought leaders are helping people live more deliberately.

Finally, Carl Jung's ideas and self–realization efforts helped to inspire the activities that follow. Jung, like Thoreau, actively experimented with living deliberately. The fruits of Jung's experiments found their way into his own life journey, as well as into the lives of people who sought his assistance with their self–realization efforts.

As you proceed through the following activities, please remember the ancient Eastern advice for anyone embarking on a path of self–realization: *The journey is the goal.* Being on the path is what matters, not how far you have come or far you suspect there may be to go. Learn from your current experiments in living deliberately, and avoid evaluating your progress by comparing yourself with others who also may be on a journey. Be content to be on the journey. *Let that become your goal.*

Remember these thoughts as you conduct your experiments

Life is an experiment, the more experiments, the better.

Ralph Waldo Emerson

If one appears to have failed, he should realize that there are no failures in the Universe...Failure is a false thought...it is a belief in limitations that do not exist.

Ernest Holmes, *The Science of Mind*

• You are conducting experiments. The goal is to learn from *whatever* you experience. "Failure" is only a belief that you cannot learn from your experiences.

PREVIEW OF ACTIVITIES

• **Experiments in Living Deliberately** — activities that develop the concept of living more deliberately as we apply spiritual principles in our daily activities

• **Experiments in Simplifying Our Lives** — activities that assist in removing unnecessary mental and physical clutter from our lives and help us distinguish between necessities and luxuries

• **Experiments in Re–allying Ourselves with Nature** — activities that help activate our senses and empower them to discern Spirit in Nature and to create bonds between ourselves and Nature's spiritual energies

EXPERIMENTS IN LIVING DELIBERATELY

"I know of no more encouraging fact than the unquestionable ability of man to elevate his life by a conscious endeavor."

Walden

"The beginning of personal transformation is absurdly easy. We only have to pay attention to the flow of attention itself. Immediately we have added a new perspective. Mind can then observe its many moods, its body tensions, the flux of attention, its choices and impasses."

Marilyn Ferguson, *The Aquarian Conspiracy*

PREVIEW: Living Deliberately

- **Keep a Journal**
- **Live Mindfully**
- **Take Control of Your Thoughts**
- **Earn a "Right Livelihood"**
- **Understand Money**
- **Nurture a Spiritual Awakening**

One of Thoreau's greatest contributions to humanity was his determination to live deliberately—*to apply spiritual principles in his daily activities.* His search for how to live more deliberately can assist in your own journey toward self–realization. Several of the following activities for living deliberately were inspired by Thoreau's efforts and the impact they had upon my own personal journey during the past two decades. The first two activities, the journal and mindfulness, are preliminary steps for living more deliberately. The journal will stimulate enhanced awareness as you progress upon your journey, and mindfulness will furnish insights to help you apply spiritual principles to your daily needs. These two resources will become powerful allies in your attempt to live more deliberately.

Preliminary Experiment

Before beginning your journey into living more deliberately, however, take a few minutes to write down your thoughts and impressions about what "living deliberately" means to you *right now.*

- List any words or phrases that come into your awareness as you explore this idea. If you feel you need help in getting started, you may want to review Thoreau's thoughts on human nature that were presented in Part One.

- Periodically, as you continue upon your journey toward living deliberately, refer to these initial thoughts and impressions. Record any new insights that have surfaced since you began your journey. Most likely, you will find that periodic feedback enhances your experience of *life as a journey* and provides new perspectives useful in living more deliberately in the future.

EXPERIMENT ONE: KEEP A JOURNAL

> "I keep a journal which should contain those thoughts and impressions which I am most liable to forget that I had."
>
> Thoreau, *Journals*

Virtually anyone who has developed his or her potential to great heights could present the merits of keeping a journal, since there appears to be a strong correlation between keeping a journal and nurturing our highest potential. Thoreau, however, not only *kept* a journal, he did it with an almost unparalleled passion and zeal. Thoreau's *Journals*, an extraordinary collection containing more than two million words, are America's most extensive record of one person's life experiences. Quantity was not his only strength, as Martin Buber indicates: "By speaking as concretely as he does about his own historical situation, Thoreau expresses exactly that which is valid for all human history."

- **Thoreau, the exemplary journal–keeper, will be our guide for keeping a journal.**

Consider Thoreau's own thoughts about keeping a journal:

> We should not endeavor coolly to analyze our thoughts, but, keeping the pen even and parallel with the current, make an accurate transcript of them. Impulse is, after all, the best linguist.
>
> *Journal*, 1838

> My journal is a record of the mellow and ripe moments that I would keep. I do not preserve the husk of life, but the kernel.
>
> *Journal*, 1851

I keep a journal which should contain those thoughts and impressions which I am most liable to forget that I had.

Journal, 1851

I can hardly believe that there is so great a difference between one year and another as my journal shows.

Journal, 1851

Time never passes so rapidly as when I am engaged in recording my thoughts.

Journal, 1852

Thoreau's own ideas on keeping a journal present several incentives for keeping our own journal including the following:

- To stimulate more thought by writing down our ideas

- To stimulate immediate "intuitive" impressions

- To encourage self-knowledge

- To avoid judgment of our thoughts before we have had time to express them fully

- To harvest the choice ideas (the "kernels") from our many life experiences

- To provide a permanent record of our thoughts, so we do not lose them through time

- To provide perspective on our thoughts and lives as we review prior journal entries

- To promote awareness of the present moment

- To engage ourselves in an engrossing, rewarding activity

- Can you add other ideas or insights from your own experience?

Aha! Thoreau intuited the value of journaling

Contemporary human potential researchers have found that keeping a journal actually stimulates and nurtures the creative processes listed above, largely because journal keeping promotes self–awareness and a broader perspective upon our lives. Through time, your journal will become a collection of your own thoughts, ideas, and impressions. As discussed below, your journal also will be an excellent location to record your thoughts and impressions concerning your personal experiments in living deliberately. For these reasons, keeping a journal contributes substantially to our progress in life's journey.

Suggestions for Keeping a Journal

Use the following suggestions if you have little experience in keeping a journal or if you desire to expand your present journal–keeping to include studying the wisdom great minds such as Thoreau have provided us. Initially, until journal–keeping becomes a familiar and comfortable experience, commit yourself to making **daily** journal entries, no matter how small or trivial they seem. Remember, your journal is a spontaneous reflection upon your own life experiences; therefore, maintain an open mind and avoid judgment and criticism of your entries. Through time, you most likely will find that you no longer need a *commitment* to journal–keeping, because keeping a journal will have become a stimulating and rewarding activity. Use your imagination and trust your intuitive hunches as you try the suggestions listed below.

Journal Suggestions

1. Write a "letter" to Thoreau or any other "great mind" that:

- will ask questions or seek advice from the great mind

- will offer your comments, suggestions, and feedback to the great mind

- will tell the person how an idea he or she produced has affected you

- will ask how a great mind's most important observations developed

- will show how you have related one of the great mind's ideas to another person's ideas

- will be a letter of introduction to introduce yourself to a great mind or to introduce one great mind to another

2. Construct imaginary dialogues to explore ideas:

- between yourself and great minds   (example below)

You: "Socrates, if you believed so much in the potential goodness of humanity and that humans are capable of great things, why were you not more active to end slavery and the subjugation of women in Athens in your day?"

Socrates: "Athens was not ready for many departures from the elitist mentality from which Pericles led us. We simply did not have sufficient perspective upon ourselves to see that Athenian citizenship should include all in our midst, not just those whose power had been traditionally recognized. In spite of our shortcomings, at least we made a small contribution to the evolution of consciousness, something present generations often forget while caught in their materialistic stupor."

- dialogues between two or more great minds (for example: between Thoreau and Buddha, Emerson and St. Teresa, or Mozart, Lao Tzu, Gertrude Stein, and Aristotle, etc.)

3. Plan a trip to visit Thoreau's or another great mind's era:

- describe what you would like to see and do in that era

- describe what you could bring with you as a hospitality gift to your host

- list a few items you would bring to inform the great mind about your own era

- select a few people you would take with you and explain why you chose them

4. Prepare a thank you note to a great mind for his or her contributions to your personal journey

5. Imagine that Thoreau or other great minds ask your advice on a situation and form a response to their request

6. Determine what you "really want in life," your highest goals and: a) compare these with what you feel were the goals held by different great minds b) compare strategies for reaching your goals with those of great minds having similar goals — what can you learn from their efforts

EXPERIMENT TWO: LIVE MINDFULLY

"The highest mental practice is to listen to the Inner Voice and to declare Its Presence."

Ernest Holmes, *The Science of Mind*

"No method nor discipline can supersede the necessity of being forever on the alert."

Thoreau, *Walden*

PREVIEW: Experiments in Living Mindfully

- **Reduce Daydreaming**
- **Cultivate Mindfulness**
- **Meditate to Focus on the Truth Within**

• REDUCE DAYDREAMING

> "Thoreau always lived each moment of the
> day...this granted him great wisdom."

Emerson's Essay, "Thoreau"

Daydreaming, even though it can be quite imaginative and stimulating, almost without exception begins as a way to gratify some unfulfilled ego–need. We allow daydreaming to replace mindful attention to our present life experience, often without even being aware that we have done so. Our attention leaves mindfulness of our current environment to grasp for some unfulfilled need we mistakenly believe dwells in the past or in the future. We replay the past either to escape to some previous experience that we found desirable or to badger ourselves with our prior mistakes and failures. We create future scenarios to escape from the present experience into a time we hope will be more desirable or prosperous than our current surroundings.

Allowing our mind to jump into the past or future is highly counterproductive to developing mindfulness. In addition, because daydreaming chiefly operates in behalf of our "selfish" ego needs —*not our higher self*— it is fantasy in service of the ego's needs. We must cultivate appreciation for whatever we currently experience, because that experience is reality. Activities to reduce idle daydreaming include:

Activity — Keep a Daydream Log

Keep a log for a whole day (or at least 8 hours) that reflects any daydreaming you experience. Whenever you find yourself daydreaming, record your experience in the daydream log as soon as possible.

1. Note in your log the following items related to each daydream incidence:

- what you were doing immediately prior to beginning to daydream

- what you did the moment you were aware you were daydreaming

- whether the daydream centered upon the past or the future

- your emotional response to the daydream (happy, anxious, curious, etc.)

- how easily you returned from daydreaming to other activities

2. At the end of the day, review your daydream log and consider the following items:

- look for "daydream triggers" — your activities immediately prior to each daydreaming experience; notice if there are similarities among your "triggers"

- determine if you tended to daydream more about the past or the future and what this may tell you

- notice your emotional responses to each daydream and how it affected your daily activities and life experience

- notice if it was easy or difficult to return to other activities from each experience and what this may indicate

3. Review your log and write down your observations and impressions. Occasionally, perform another daydream log activity for a whole day. Compare your experiences. What do you notice? Many people have found that this activity assists them in gaining control over idle daydreaming and helps them live more deliberately.

NOTE: the goal of this experiment is to become more mindful — not to eliminate daydreaming altogether. Even a small increase in our control over daydreaming yields benefits in living more deliberately. For example, we will provide ourselves with the opportunity to *choose* whether we wish to continue a daydream or to return to being mindful of our other activities, an important *choice* needed for living more deliberately. We also will become more aware of how often we actually do daydream. Finally, we can discover where our mind tends to "go" in search of the ego–fulfillment it believes it will find in a daydream reality. The following activity also will develop mindfulness.

• CULTIVATE MINDFULNESS — "WASHING THE DISHES TO WASH THE DISHES"

Eastern master Thich Nhat Hanh teaches his pupils the value of developing mindfulness as they perform their daily activities. He gives them the example of "washing the dishes to wash the dishes." Because most of us see little value in thinking about washing dishes, we disengage our minds from the process of washing dishes and may think about something completely different: the book we are reading, a past experience in which we acted improperly, some problem we must solve at the office, or a host of other potential distractions from the present moment. We avoid the present experience and hope that something else we could think about will help us tolerate the drudgery of the present task. For the moment, we are not "alive."

If letting our minds wander in this manner were only an occasional response to such activities, we might not need to cultivate mindfulness through practicing various techniques. Unfortunately, because we seldom realize how easily our minds flee from our daily activities and escape to other activities, we nurture a wandering mind, not mindfulness. It does not matter whether our minds flee to "desirable" thoughts (solving problems, recalling special moments, etc.) or "undesirable" thoughts (our past failures, problems we cannot seem to solve, wishing that things would somehow get better, etc.), because we have encouraged mindlessness in both instances. If we desire to encourage mindfulness, then we must devote conscious effort to "washing the dishes to wash the dishes." We must learn to stay centered upon our present experiences, no matter how mundane or unchallenging we may perceive them to be.

We can nurture mindfulness as we perform a few of our daily tasks or activities. We each have numerous tasks that we must perform as part of our daily activities. These tasks will provide an excellent opportunity for disciplining our minds and staying mindful of the present experience. Use the following guidelines to help you cultivate mindfulness as you perform daily tasks.

1. Select an activity that you frequently must perform and in which you ordinarily let your mind wander as you perform it. Also, it helps to select one that does not take more than a few minutes to perform until you have had experience with creating mindfulness in this manner. Once you have developed a degree of mindfulness during shorter tasks, move on to longer tasks. Examples of such activities include:

• washing the dishes	• changing the kitty litter
• brushing your teeth	• filling the car with gas
• taking a shower	• peeling vegetables
• waiting in line	• brushing your hair
• taking out the trash	• walking the dog

2. As you perform the activity, devote your full attention to the activity. Focus upon the physical sensations you experience, the bodily actions you are using, the steps you must take to perform the activity, and any other elements that directly connect your awareness with the experience. In other words, "become one with the activity," as if there were nothing else in the whole universe except you and this activity.

3. If any thoughts other than those directly related to your activity creep in, **let them go** as soon as you have become aware of them. If you follow them any longer than your first awareness of them, then you will have reinforced a wandering mind and strengthened mind-lessness. As soon as you have let go of a distracting thought, simply return your awareness to performing the activity. Repeat this process each time you encounter a thought that would distract you from mindful awareness. Remember, you can *choose* where your attention settles.

4. Once you have finished the activity, note your immediate sensations and impressions. Record them in your journal, if you like. Through time, you probably will discover that you have improved your mental discipline by becoming mindful as you perform life's necessary, but mundane, tasks.

• MEDITATE — *LEARN TO FOCUS UPON THE TRUTH WITHIN YOURSELF*

"If with closed ears and eyes I consult consciousness for a moment, immediately are all walls and barriers dissipated, earth rolls from under me...I dissolve all lesser lights into my own intenser and steadier light."

Thoreau, *Journals*

What is meditation?

Meditation is an activity in which people can expand their awareness in a step–by–step manner. In both Eastern and Western cultures, many people have used the expanded awareness that meditation produces to develop their full mental and spiritual potential.

For our purposes, meditation will mean a distinct period of **no less than fifteen minutes** when we will quiet our minds and concentrate our full attention within ourselves to seek inspiration, insight, or union with the Universal Mind or God. Once we learn to meditate in these short sessions, then we are prepared to extend our meditative awareness into our daily activities or while we are in Nature, as did Thoreau.

Demonstrated Benefits of Meditation

- increased creativity
- improved problem-solving
- improved self-discipline
- fewer negative thoughts

- overcoming irrational fears
- improved self-concept
- many physiological benefits
- greater spiritual awareness

Above from: *Your Maximum Mind* by Dr. Herbert Benson
Director of Behavioral Medicine at Harvard Medical School

STEP ONE: CALMING THE MIND
WITH RELAXATION TECHNIQUES

GOAL: To prepare for meditation by slowing the mind down from its usual pace maintained during ordinary waking consciousness.

The technique of resting the mind and the power of
dismissing from it all care and worry is probably one
of the secrets of energy in all great people.

J. A. Hadfield

The ability to relax the body and mind from its normal
attentiveness to internal and external stimuli and to our
thought processes is an important first step in meditation.
Dr. Herbert Benson and other researchers have demonstrated
numerous positive effects that relaxation techniques have
upon the body and mind. Benson indicates that once we
relax our mind, it pays less attention to potential distractions
and demonstrates greater potential for meditative awareness.
His work also indicated that the routine inner dialogue of our
ordinary waking consciousness interferes with meditation.
We must realize that ordinary waking consciousness'
tendency to evaluate, judge, and categorize our experiences
is a formidable barrier to achieving the inner calmness
needed during meditation. There are, however, factors that
facilitate relaxation including the ones listed below.

Four Factors Enhancing Relaxation

1. A quiet environment — this reduces the mind's
natural efforts to "danger–scan" any sounds it picks up. This
learned response serves to protect us from potential dangers
by alerting us and then prompting us to focus attention upon
the source of the sound to determine if there is an imminent
danger. A quiet environment helps reduce this potential
distraction to relaxation. Also, direct your telephone calls to
an answering machine or switch off the ringing mechanism
to avoid this potential interruption. Once you have learned to
relax in a quiet environment, try meditation in natural
settings.

2. A passive attitude — it would be counter-productive if our efforts to induce relaxation would themselves become a source of tension. The key to maintaining a passive attitude is to hold no preconceived ideas about how you *should* feel. Each meditation session is a unique experience; therefore, there is no "right" or "wrong" meditative experience. You may find it helpful to avoid forcing your thoughts in any particular direction or holding on to any particular sensation or thought that you experience. Through time and with patience you may notice that your thoughts slow down on their own.

3. A comfortable position — one in which the body feels no particular physical stress. In most cases, sitting in a comfortable chair with your feet on the floor is best. Your arms can either be in your lap, by your side, or placed upon the chair arms. Move yourself around to find a position so that you feel like an "old rag doll"—*loose and relaxed.* Some people meditate while laying upon their backs. You also may use this position, provided you do not fall asleep often.

4. "Seating Practices" — specific actions to promote a sense of significance for the meditative session. Eastern meditation practices, as well as many Western religious rituals, place considerable importance upon the *spiritual atmosphere* that is conducive for meditation and contemplation. Creating an environment—both a physical and a mental environment—conducive to meditation helps us recognize and appreciate the importance of meditation in our lives. This facilitates the transition from ordinary daily activities to meditative states of awareness and helps us maintain those states once we experience them. **Factors useful in creating the spiritual atmosphere include:**

• *The meditation sanctuary* Reserve a special location for meditation or other activities such as reading related to spiritual matters. This will be your primary meditative sanctuary, although other places also can become your sanctuary. Many people such as Thoreau, Emerson, O'Keeffe, and Beethoven used Nature as their sanctuary. Thoreau and Emerson could spent long hours in a mindful and reverent communion with Nature which was a form of meditation. Likewise, Beethoven and O'Keeffe often retreated to the countryside for long leisurely walks. On many occasions they returned from their meditative sessions in Nature with a new musical or artistic composition dancing in their minds.

• *Create an environment conducive to meditation.* Use art, symbols, pictures, sounds, smells, colors, etc. that you find promote a sense of reverence. Nature is an excellent place for meditation, once you have developed the ability to relax and center your mind.

• *Daily meditation* One of the most important seating practices is to treat meditation as a special, yet daily, activity. Have a regular time for your primary meditation session and let nothing interfere with it. Of course you may meditate more than once a day, but at least one of those times should be a special, more reverent meditation session.

PRELIMINARY RELAXATION EXERCISE: THREE DEEP BREATHS

GOAL: To develop a mental "trigger" to facilitate meditative awareness.

One of the most remarkable things about the human brain is that it can learn to respond to experiences that it frequently encounters without having to *think* about responding. For example, we have encountered stop signs in our driving to such an extent that we no longer have to think: "There is a stop sign. I must place my right foot on the brake petal and stop the car." Instead, we simply stop the car without devoting conscious attention to the process, because the sign has triggered a response. We will use the brain's ability to respond to frequently encountered experiences to our advantage in the meditation process with an activity known as Three Deep Breaths.

PLEASE NOTE: This is a preliminary activity for all meditation sessions

1. Once you have "seated" yourself according to the suggestions above, close your eyes and relax for a minute. Just let the mind and body relax without paying attention to any particular thought or sensation.

2. Next, **slowly** inhale through your nose. Continue to inhale slowly and pay attention to the air as it comes into your nostrils. Focus your full attention to the air as it enters. Feel the air filling your lungs and feel your chest expanding as you continue to fill your lungs to a full, but comfortable level. You also may notice that your shoulders rise slightly as you fill your lungs with air. Once your lungs are full, hold your breath for a moment. Do not hold it until it becomes uncomfortable, just until you have felt the fullness of your lungs for a few moments.

3. Now **slowly** let the air pass from your lungs out through slightly parted lips. Feel the air as it leaves your lungs and feel it passing out through your lips. Also, pay attention to how your shoulders may be lowering themselves and how you may feel as if you were sinking down into the chair. Continue to let the air out slowly until you feel you have emptied your lungs of air. Then

pull in your stomach muscles slightly and push out a little more air. Feel the air leaving your lungs.

4. Once you have pushed all the air out of your lungs, repeat the cycle. Inhale slowly, hold it (a little longer this time), and let it out completely. Pay full attention to the sensations of breathing in this manner as you complete the cycle. Once you have completed the second deep breath cycle, repeat for one more cycle.

5. After finishing the third deep breath, keep your eyes closed and enjoy the sensations you experience for a minute or two. Let your mind follow your breathing as it returns to its ordinary pace. Relax for a few moments before continuing with the meditation session.

6. Through time, you will have developed the **Three Deep Breaths** as your "trigger" to relax. Then you will notice that simply taking the three breaths and following the accompanying sensations will take you into a state in which your mind and body are very relaxed. Until that time, however, you most likely will need to perform an additional relaxation activity such as the **Relaxing Image** which follows.

How will I know if I'm relaxed?

The answer to this question varies considerably, as each of us has a different understanding and experience of relaxation. For our purposes, **relaxation is a state in which you might notice:**

• that there is a reduced need to shift the body in order to feel comfortable

• that your mind does not "race" but seems to "flow" gently from sensation to sensation

• that you rarely, if at all, become concerned with noises or other external sensations

• that your perception of time seems to slow down or disappear; time becomes "irrelevant"

If you feel that you are relaxed, then either proceed to **Step Two** or return to your daily activities using the procedure for departing relaxed states of awareness presented at the conclusion of the **Relaxing Image** technique. If you feel that you are not relaxed, then use the following exercise to deepen your relaxation.

Be patient! Learning to relax takes time and practice. If your session progresses no further than your experiencing a light degree of relaxation, be thankful! Even a slight departure from the day's often hectic pace will benefit you and your attempts to live more deliberately.

DEEPENING YOUR RELAXATION: THE RELAXING IMAGE

GOAL: To create a multi-sensory mental image to promote deeper states of relaxation.

If after the **Three Deep Breaths** you do not feel adequately relaxed, then use the **Relaxing Image** to deepen your relaxation. Continue to keep your eyes shut and avoid moving your body as much as possible. Allow the image to form in your mind without forcing it or expecting to experience it in any certain manner.

1. Imagine a setting in which you might find yourself relaxed simply by being there. Allow the image to form in your mind without forcing it. Once an image appears, begin to add sensory details to enhance its clarity. Adding sensory details to a mental image strengthens the image in

our "mind's eye" and helps the mind focus more upon it than upon our present setting and its potential distractions. As you are using your imagination, it really does not matter if you have ever been to a particular setting to create a relaxing image based upon that setting. Remember, the only limits to the unlimited power of your imagination are those you *choose* to set.

Suggestions for relaxing images and accompanying multi–sensory details include:

Adding Multi–sensory Details

A FIELD IN THE COUNTRYSIDE

- smell of fresh grass or flowers
- sound of birds chirping or singing
- sight of white, puffy clouds in a deep blue sky
- texture of the grass or other objects

THE PORCH OF A MOUNTAIN CABIN

- sight of a beautiful vista
- smell of cedar trees and clean, fresh air
- texture of the cabin's wood
- sound of the wind whistling in the trees

A WARM, SUNNY DAY AT THE BEACH

- sound of the waves, sea gulls, seashells
- smell of the salty air
- sight of sailboats gliding upon the water
- texture of the sand or a seashell

A "SAFE HAVEN"

• anyplace you can create sensory details that make you feel comfortable and relaxed

2. Once you have created your image and have begun to experience the setting in a multi–sensory fashion, just relax for a few minutes. Your mind, by providing multi–sensory details to it, will respond to the image as if you were really there enjoying the relaxation of that setting. Continue to experience the image until you feel very relaxed (refer to the suggestions presented above for determining relaxation). If your mind wanders off to other images or thoughts, simply let those impressions go as soon as you are aware of their presence. Then refocus upon the relaxing image. Your mind may wander frequently at first; however, with practice and patience, you will find that it will remain centered upon the relaxing image for an extended period of time.

3. Once you feel very relaxed, you have several options:

• to continue relaxing either by remaining in the relaxing image or by sitting quietly with your eyes closed and your mind focused upon no particular thought or impression

• to move to **Step Two** which is presented below

• to prepare for sleep

• to return to your daily activities (see procedure below)

Procedure for Leaving Relaxed or Meditative States of Awareness

Entry into relaxed or meditative states of awareness is a gradual process involving several steps. Likewise, departing from these states and returning to active waking consciousness also must be a gradual, step–by–step process. This will help you retain the benefits (your relaxation, the insights you received, or your increased self–awareness) you have obtained during the meditative session. When you feel that it is time to return to active waking consciousness, prepare to leave meditative awareness in the following steps:

1. Silently count backwards from the number five to the number one in a slow, rhythmic manner. When you reach the number one, silently repeat the following or a similar expression: "I am refreshed, relaxed, and mentally alert." When you complete the expression, slowly open your eyes.

2. Draw in a slow, deep breath through your nostrils and then exhale it as if it were a big sigh. Move your feet around a bit and then stretch your arms if you like.

3. If appropriate, record in your journal any impressions or insights you have gleaned from your meditative experience before returning to other activities.

STEP TWO: CLEARING THE MIND BY DISCIPLINING TECHNIQUES

GOAL: From the *Bhagavadgita* — "To hold the senses and imagination in check and to keep the mind concentrated upon its object."

Consider the following thoughts for a moment

> Those divine sounds which are uttered to our inward ear—which are breathed in with the zephyr—come to us noiselessly, bathing the temples of the soul, as we stand motionless.
>
> Thoreau, *Journals*

> The mind is flighty and elusive, moving wherever it pleases. Taming it is wonderful indeed — for a disciplined mind invites true joy.
>
> Buddha, *Dhammapada*

> The faculty of voluntarily bringing back a wandering attention over and over again is at the very root of judgment, character, and will. No one is *compos sui* if he does not have it. An education which improves this faculty would be an education par excellence.
>
> William James, *Principles of Psychology*

Do you notice any similarities among these thoughts? One common element could be that each addresses our greatest barrier to developing meditative awareness—*the tendency of our mind to wander*. Perhaps you have experienced the frustration of possessing a wandering mind when a task called for a disciplined mental focus. Few of us have been taught to focus our minds upon one single subject for an extended period in order to reduce the mind's tendency to wander. If we desire to develop meditative awareness and to receive its contribution to living deliberately, then we must nurture a well–disciplined mind— *both during meditation sessions and in our daily activities.*

DISCIPLINING METHODS PRIMARILY USED *DURING* MEDITATION SESSIONS

Open Eye Contemplation

Paul Cézanne maintained that "observation modifies vision." His insight confirms what experienced meditators from Eastern and Western civilizations have known for thousands of years — *that the very act of seeing alters how we see.* Long before Cézanne used the principle of disciplined observation to help art move to new levels of expression, Christian mystic St. Teresa of Avila used this principle to teach her students how to obtain the mental discipline necessary for meditation. She wrote, "I do not require of you to form great and serious considerations in your thinking. I require of you only to look." Her method correlates with open eye contemplation methods that Zen masters have used for centuries to teach their students how to discipline the mind.

Open eye contemplation of an object is an excellent method to discipline a *relaxed* mind. If you have not relaxed before attempting to discipline the mind, expect a most formidable challenge. Ordinary waking consciousness, as William James indicates, tends to wander, and it must be "educated" by repeatedly returning it to a chosen path. To attempt this task with an unrelaxed mind will create frustration and tension, conditions that thwart meditative awareness. Open eye contemplation, because it places the mind upon a single path to tread, provides sufficient discipline to attain higher meditative states.

1. Select a natural object for observation. Start with objects that will fit comfortably in your hand such as a rock, twig, seashell, piece of bark, etc. Take into consideration that you will need to use the same object *daily* for at least two weeks. Staying with the same object for several weeks enhances mental discipline. You will need to practice the exercise for a minimum of five minutes during the first few weeks and later expand to ten or fifteen minutes to attain the greater discipline required by advanced meditative states.

2. Relax using the exercises and suggestions in **Step One**. After attaining a state of relaxation, place the object in your hand. Hold it in front of you at a comfortable distance from your eyes. Observe and explore it as a child would, with natural curiosity that is free from any preconceived ideas or judgments. Become fascinated with the object and bring yourself into an intimate relationship with it. Avoid *thinking* about the object: where it came from, how it might look as a piece of jewelry, how much it weighs, how pretty it is, etc. as much as possible.

The goal is to develop a focused mind that is as free from all thought as is possible. Remember, we just want to *experience* the object, not *think* about it.

3. If your mind starts to wander away from observation or begins to *think* about the object or anything else, simply return to *experiencing* the object. Do not scold yourself for drifting away, simply note that you have drifted and promptly return your mind to the object you are contemplating.

4. Once you feel your mind stays with the object for five minutes with very few wanderings or deliberations about it, expand the time to ten minutes. Once you achieve proficiency at this longer time period, change to a new object and explore it for ten minutes. If you experience difficulty, cut the time back to five minutes and work back up to ten.

5. Once you achieve proficiency with objects found in Nature, experiment with other objects such as simple line drawings or spiritual symbols and images. These objects require more concentration than you might think, so save them until you are quite proficient with simple natural objects.

Counting Breaths

Counting your "out-breaths" or exhalations is a method for disciplining the mind used for several thousand years in many cultures. For example, Zen masters have used breathing exercises to help their students overcome the distractions to meditation so often generated by the verbal, conscious mind. When students report distractions, especially imagery of an alluring nature which leads away from proper disciplining of the mind, the masters tell their students: "If you concentrate upon your breathing, the distractions will go away."

Counting breaths is simple and easy to learn; yet, it is one of the most powerful and effective methods available to help us overcome the distractions of our ordinary consciousness. The goal is to experience—*to become one with*—your own breathing by counting each exhalation. You simply pay full attention to the counting process and direct attention away from thoughts, sensations, feelings, and other distractions. If your mind strays from counting, gently return it to the counting process.

1. After attaining a relaxed state, sit in a comfortable, erect position. Initially devote five minutes to practicing this technique after your relaxing activities. Continue to practice it during each meditation session until you are able to complete five to ten minutes with minimal distractions.

2. Close your eyes and begin to breathe in full, deep breaths in and out through your nose. Let a slow, natural rhythm develop before you begin to count. *Feel* the air coming in and going out. Pay full attention to your breathing process. Once you feel a rhythm, begin counting each exhalation.

3. Count each separate exhalation until you get to four. Once you have exhaled four times and have reached a count of four, start over at one. Continue counting in the cycle up to four for the duration of the session.

If your mind strays, do not worry. Simply return to the counting at either the number you last remember or at one. Also, try to maintain the natural rhythm you established before beginning the counting process. Varying the rhythm is a source of distraction. Remember: *Experience your breathing!*

Following Sounds

Another way to discipline the mind is through your sense of hearing. This method works especially well in Nature, once you have developed sufficient discipline that your mind does not wander easily. Your goal is to listen fully and attentively to the sound and keep your mind focused upon it. Experience the sound with an open mind so that you become "one with it" as in the open eye disciplining exercise above. If your mind drifts away, simply refocus upon the sound and continue. You may want to close your eyes to concentrate upon the sound. Practice following sounds for five minutes at first and later increase your concentration to ten minutes. Sounds which promote mental discipline include:

Wind chimes: If you can attain a relaxed state outdoors, sit in it in a location where you will hear the sound of wind chimes. Follow the sounds produced by the chimes with your full attention.

Moving Water: Sit by a rushing stream or river and listen attentively to the sound of moving water. If you can maintain sufficient mental focus in an urban environment, sitting by fountains may help develop mental discipline.

Beach: Find a sparsely populated area of the beach and listen to Nature's symphony: surf, sea gulls, ocean breeze, etc.

Forest: Find a place in which you will feel comfortable and listen attentively to the diverse natural sounds around you.

Bird Songs: One of the most enjoyable natural sounds is that of birds singing. Find a place in which you may encounter a variety of birds and listen attentively.

Heartbeat

This disciplining technique focuses attention upon one of our many natural rhythms—*the heartbeat*. The heart provides us with an "inner metronome" that we can use to promote discipline during meditation. As you sit quietly after relaxing the mind, direct your attention inwards to your heartbeat. Concentrate your awareness upon this inner rhythm and let all other sensations pass away. Become one with this inner rhythm.

If you have difficulty locating your heartbeat among the myriad internal sensations, place your fingers upon your wrist as medical personnel do to locate your pulse. Feel the pulsing rhythm with your fingers and let it stimulate awareness of your heartbeat. Focus your full attention on the sensations produced by your heart. Pay full attention to this rhythm for a few minutes to enhance mental discipline and prepare the mind for further meditation.

PLEASE NOTE : Any of the above techniques may be practiced at times *other than during* your meditation session to enhance mental discipline both for meditation and for other activities. Find the particular techniques that seem to work best for you. Additional techniques follow that can be used *outside* your meditation sessions to promote mental discipline.

DISCIPLINING METHODS PRIMARILY USED *OTHER THAN DURING* MEDITATION SESSIONS

We can enhance mental discipline during meditation sessions substantially through the inclusion of a few disciplining techniques *in our other daily activities*. We can hardly discipline our often unruly mind effectively if we attempt to do so only during meditation sessions. Generating sufficient discipline to calm the mind during meditation requires more frequent attention.

The Ripple Effect

The benefits of disciplining the mind during our ordinary daily activities will ripple over into our meditation sessions and *vice versa*. Not only will disciplining activities performed as part of our daily life enhance mental discipline during meditation, but it also will assist us in our other daily activities.

If you ever have found your mind wandering during problem-solving, reading, conversation, watching a movie, or other activities, then you most likely are aware of the need to provide yourself with more mental discipline. Developing mental discipline is an investment in ourselves. This investment will pay off both during meditation and your other daily activities, because our minds will be focused fully and completely upon our tasks and problem–solving activities. Enhanced mental discipline, therefore, will increase your overall productivity and effectiveness. We nurture mental discipline simply by adding a few easily practiced techniques to our daily schedule.

Attentive Driving

Most of us have had the experience of driving our cars as if we were operating under the influence of some unseen "automatic pilot." We lose mindfulness of what we are doing as we explore our thoughts, hold conversations, daydream, etc. Rarely do we devote significant attention to the actual processes and activities that are involved in driving our car. This exercise enhances our mental discipline during the longer tasks we face such as driving the car.

First, determine that you will use attentive driving *before* you get into the car. Try using it with a short trip that is not during rush hour or in heavy traffic. (It sounds ludicrous that we shouldn't consider paying full attention to what we are doing in heavy traffic, but as we have become so accustomed to driving without thinking, anything different may seem most alien to us and could serve as a distraction.) Focus your full attention upon *everything* that you do from the moment you insert the key into the door. Become one with what you are doing: your body movements, the decisions that have to be made, the road in front of you, other cars, driving conditions, the vibrations from your car, etc. Keep your attention focused solely upon things related to driving your car. Reject all other thoughts to promote mental discipline.

Conscious Eating

Many times we eat without awareness of what we are doing. This not only reduces our potential enjoyment of the food and causes us to eat more than we may need, but it also encourages unfocused and undisciplined attention. As in the exercises above, we are to focus our attention fully upon what we are doing. Pay attention to the taste, smell, and texture of the food as you eat. Also concentrate upon the mechanics of eating. Become aware of selecting a bite with the fork or spoon, lifting it to your mouth, and chewing and swallowing the food. If any other thoughts come as you eat, reject them and return your full attention to eating.

• How will I know when my mind is cleared of unnecessary thoughts?

Once you have employed the disciplining techniques for use during mediation sessions, you may notice your mind is considerably more calm and centered than before you began. At this point you may want to determine if you still encounter any unnecessary thoughts and sensations which may have to be cleared before continuing with the meditative session. Suggestions for recognizing if unnecessary and potentially distracting thoughts remain include determining:

- are you more aware of your inner sensations than your outer sensations?

- are there periods when there seems to be no "thinking" at all, just "being?"

- do you quickly let go of most potentially distracting thoughts or ideas?

- do you experience deep inner peace and tranquillity?

- is your present experience comfortable, just as it is, without wanting to change anything?

If you experience several of these characteristics, then your mind, most likely, is prepared to continue with the meditative session. If not, then you may need to continue with the same disciplining technique you were employing or select another one. Do not expect to attain a calm, clear mind in every meditation session—*especially in your initial meditative experiences.* It may take considerable practice to attain a centered mind in your meditation sessions. Be patient and diligent in your efforts.

• **Now that I'm centered, what do I do?**

Once you realize that you have cleared your mind through the disciplining techniques, you may continue with your pre–determined purpose for the session including:

- staying in the calm, clear awareness you now experience; simply enjoying "being in the moment"

- using affirmations to promote a more positive mental framework (for ideas, see experiment six in this chapter)

- using guided visualization exercises (either taped exercises or ones you have learned)

- returning to waking consciousness using the departure technique described above

---

EXPERIMENT THREE: TAKE CONTROL OF YOUR THOUGHTS

"Man is the artifice of his own happiness. Let him beware how he complains of the disposition of circumstances, for it is his own disposition he blames."

Thoreau, *Journals*

> "We are all immersed in the atmosphere of our own thinking, which is the direct result of all we have ever said, thought, or done."

Ernest Holmes, *The Science of Mind*

Many people state that they sometimes find themselves attending to trivial thoughts, fears, or expectations when they know it would be more appropriate to avoid these useless and counterproductive thoughts. We acquired many of these habitual or routine thoughts and fears from the people around us as we matured. We noticed that they seemed concerned with these thoughts and often expressed them to others. Most likely, we assumed that we, too, should have such thoughts as part of our life experience.

These trivial thoughts not only are unnecessary, but they also can profane the mind and become an addiction, as Thoreau observed. Contemporary psychological researchers confirm what Eastern and Western mystics through the ages have maintained — *our minds create reality*. If our mind attends to trivial thoughts, then we trivialize reality. We also limit our potential to live deliberately.

As Marilyn Ferguson observed in *The Aquarian Conspiracy*, we can take control of our minds—*we actually can fine–tune our awareness*. The following activities will provide opportunities for you to witness your own trivial thoughts as a preliminary step in reducing their frequency. Once you become aware of these thoughts, you will hold the power of *choice* over them. Greater awareness leads to more choices about how we live. That is living deliberately!

As you develop mindfulness of these trivial thoughts in your own life, most likely you also will notice how frequently others attend to such psychic junk food.

Remember, however, they are responsible for their own realities, and you cannot "do their work for them." Accept their present reality just as it is. Your living more deliberately may be—*in itself*—all they need to recognize the truth.

Activity — CHOICE STATEMENTS

"As a man thinks, so he is, and as a man chooses, so is he and so is nature."

Ralph Waldo Emerson, Essay, "Spiritual Laws"

"We can choose what we wish to experience."

Ernest Holmes, *The Science of Mind*

1. DEALING WITH *"I SHOULD..."*

- First, prepare a list of as many of the "shoulds" that you often repeat to yourself or others. For example: "I should spend more time exercising" or "I should not be so hasty to judge others." List as many of these thoughts as you can. Once you feel the list covers your "shoulds," start at the beginning of the list and rewrite each "should" so that it now reads: "I could........., but I have a choice." For example, instead of saying, "I *should* spend more time exercising," you would write, "I *could* spend more time exercising, but I have a choice." Rewrite each of the "shoulds" on your list in this manner emphasizing that you have a choice in the matter.

- Once you finish, review each item and read the revised idea *aloud*. Are you conscious of any changes in your feelings about this item? What does this tell you? Explore for a few minutes your immediate thoughts and feelings about rewriting these statements emphasizing your choice. Record your insights in your journal.

• The next time you find yourself thinking "I should" about a particular situation, stop for a moment, create a **choice statement**—a statement emphasizing that you have a choice in the matter—and then make your decision about the situation. Practice this process until it becomes an automatic response to generate choices—not habitual "should reactions"—to your encounters. Through time, you will discover that your life is filled with numerous possibilities for growth and expansion of your abilities. That is the power of choice statements, a power that grows with each use.

2. DEALING WITH *"I'M WORRIED ABOUT..."*

• Use the procedure above with items that create fear or worry. For example, "I am worried about saying something silly that will embarrass me." Create a choice statement as a response to the fear or anxiety: "I allow myself to worry about......, but I have a choice." Your revised list would then read: "I allow myself to worry about saying something stupid, but I have a choice." Note in your journal your feelings and thoughts as you read aloud the revised list of potential fears.

3. DEALING WITH *"I'M MAD ABOUT..."*

• Create a list with situations that frustrate you or to which you create an anger response. For example: "I get angry when I am caught in traffic" becomes, "I allow myself to get angry when I am caught in traffic, but I have a choice." Create choice statements for each of the situations and say them aloud. Focus your attention upon the immediate feelings and thoughts that this exercise produces. Practice this technique to generate awareness that our reactions to life experiences always are our *choice.*

EXPERIMENT FOUR:
EARN A "RIGHT LIVELIHOOD"

"There is little or nothing to be remembered written on the subject of getting an honest living, of how to make the getting of our living poetic! For if it is not poetic, it is not life but death we get."

Thoreau, *Journals*

"There is no more factual blunderer than he who consumes the greater part of his life getting his living...You must get your living by loving."

Thoreau, *Life Without Principle*

One of the most difficult questions that Thoreau faced was that of how we should earn a living. He observed that many people in his day earned their living through an assortment of dull, monotonous, and inherently unfulfilling jobs. He felt that their jobs, rather than inspiring them to develop their higher potential, seemed to sap their vitality and even rob them of their humanness. It seems as if little has changed since Thoreau's day. Psychologists report that many workers today are so disillusioned by the drudgery and lack of opportunity for creative expression at work that they no longer expect to find fulfillment in their jobs. They see their jobs merely as something to be tolerated in order to earn a living, not as something that contributes pleasure and meaning to life.

Is it really possible for humanity to earn its living "poetically," as Thoreau suggests? Most likely, each of us could name a few lucky souls whose occupation produced "poetic" results; however, we may doubt that virtually everyone could live in this manner. On this point, Thoreau is in accord with Buddha whose path to enlightenment contains the simple, yet profound, principle called "right livelihood."

Synthesis of Buddha's and Thoreau's Ideas

Right livelihood, as seen from a synthesis of Thoreau's and Buddha's teachings, has several elements which interact to produce harmony and balance in our total life, not just our work. The ten principles of "right livelihood" listed below apply from the most simple and basic tasks to the most demanding and challenging. These ten principles unite universal truths from the East and West into a framework that can help us live more deliberately.

Ten Principles of "Right Livelihood"

1. Work that does not bring physical harm to others

2. Work that does not involve deceit or dishonesty

3. Work that does not harm Nature

4. Work that engages our mind as well as our body

5. Work that produces beneficial or necessary products

6. Work that is harmonious with the relationships in Nature

7. Work that helps us become "one" with our tasks

8. Work that nourishes both our own and other people's creativity

9. Work that is the best possible deployment of our talents and skills

10. Work that is joyful; work that makes our life "poetic"

Activities for Applying the Principles

• THE RIGHT LIVELIHOOD SURVEY

1. Make a list of any words or phrases that you feel apply about your present job. These terms may be factual descriptions of your job (examples: involves analytical thought, demands patience, high interaction with others, bank officer, teacher, nurse, etc.) or may be your more subjective impressions of it (examples: tedious, energetic, dull, pay is too low for me, highly stimulating, etc.) Do not censor or edit your thoughts or impressions. If it enters your awareness, write it down. Be as honest as possible.

2. Place a mark beside each item on the list as follows:

   • if you feel it is a neutral, factual description, mark it "F"

   • if you feel it is an emotional or subjective description, mark it "S"

3. Next, take a blank sheet of paper and put the words "Talents and Skills" across the top. Review your list from step 1 above and then identify any items that you consider to be your present talents or skills. For our purposes, a talent or skill implies that you have the ability to perform an activity well. Your enjoyment of the activity is not a consideration for the moment, only your performance of it. Write the items you have determined to be talents or skills in the space beneath the heading.

4. Review your list of talents and skills. Determine if the majority of your talents or skills are marked as being factual or subjective descriptions. Next, write down your immediate responses to the questions that follow:

- Are most of my talents or skills factual or subjective descriptions? What does this tell me about my present talents and skills?

- What is the relationship between my talents and my present job satisfaction?

- Are there any talents that I perceive in a negative manner? What does this tell me?

- What talents do I have that are not being used by my present job? Can I apply these talents in my present job? If so, how and what response can I expect when I apply these talents? If not, are these talents crucial to my developing a sense of "poetic work" that Thoreau mentions?

5. Next, review the ten principles of "right livelihood" presented above. Write down your immediate responses to the following questions (please add your own questions, too):

- What is the relationship between my present job and "right livelihood?"

- Where am I presently most closely aligned with these principles? The furthest away from them?

- What can I do in my present job to live more in harmony with these principles?

- What barriers will I face in this endeavor, and how can I overcome them?

- Do I have allies in this endeavor? If so, how can I involve them. If not, can I create allies?

- If my present job prevents me from earning a living in accordance with the principles, then what must I do?

- What will be my first step to accomplish any of the above objectives? When will I take this step?

EXPERIMENT FIVE: UNDERSTAND "MONEY"

"The cost of a thing is the amount of what I call life which is required to be exchanged for it, immediately or in the long run."

"Money is not required to buy one necessity of the soul."

Thoreau, *Journals*

"The Material and the Spiritual are one... Property, goods, and services may all have the appearance of materiality, yet to those who understand the spiritual and mental nature of the Universe they are material *and* spiritual.

Ernest Holmes,
Practical Applications of Science of Mind

What is Money?

1. "Money" is only a state of Mind; *not a reality in, of, or for itself.* Many people often seek it as if it were the real or the only ends to be obtained through one's efforts. If money remains a state of Mind—therefore a spiritual reality—and not an end in itself, then you always will have what you truly need and deserve.

2. Money, as an energy principle of spiritual reality, naturally *flows* to us as we earn a right livelihood. Be concerned with the quality of your service you give to others, not about any rewards you may receive for the service and you will be working with the flow.

3. Money flows in unseen channels like electricity flows through wires. Because it is spiritual energy in motion, we never really have "possession" of it. To be preoccupied with possessing it to provide ourselves with security squanders our own life energy. Security is a state of Mind. It is an affirmation of the Universe's abundance.

The ideas above are adapted from:

Spiritual Economics by Eric Butterworth

The Science of Mind by Ernest Holmes

The Seven Laws of Money by Mike Phillips

Exercise in Understanding Money

Step One: Consider for a moment all the reasons why money may be important to you and other people you know. A few of the most common reasons are listed below. If you have others that are not included, please list them as well.

> 1. for security—now
>
> 2. for security—in the future
>
> 3. as a reward for a job well done
>
> 4. for freedom to do as I please
>
> 5. so I can give to my favorite charities
>
> 6. to buy the necessities of life
>
> 7. to buy things to make my life more comfortable or convenient
>
> 8. (other, please specify)

Step Two: Once you have considered these reasons and any others that you may have listed, again read and reflect upon the ideas above from Thoreau, Butterworth, Holmes, and Phillips (or others). Next, starting with the first reason why money seems to be important to people, jot down any insights that you now have about that reason in light of the principles above. What does this reason really tell me? What are the primary concerns of a person having this as a reason for money's importance? What problems might a person encounter who gives this as a reason? What sacrifices will a person believing this occasionally have to make? Will money "flow" naturally in this person's life?

Step Three: When you have finished exploring the first reason, continue with the others. After exploring all the reasons, consider what have you learned about money and your relationship with it by this exercise. List ways you can apply this information in living deliberately. Periodically review your relationship with money. (Refer to the exercises on "Living Simply" in the next chapter).

EXPERIMENT SIX: NURTURE A SPIRITUAL AWAKENING

"I would not forget that I deal with infinite and divine qualities in my fellow men. All men, indeed, are divine in their core of light."

Thoreau, *Journals*

"Never limit your view of life by any past experience. The possibility of life is inherent within the capacity to imagine what life is, backed by the power to produce this imagery, or Divine Imagination."

Ernest Holmes, *The Science of Mind*

It is pointless—*and potentially harmful*—to dwell upon the negative imagery that modern culture now beams towards us. Politicians and the mass media with their messages stressing human shortcomings in solving our fundamental problems are not the only culprits. There are even many prophets of doom within the religious ranks whose spirituality tells them that the end is near and that God's full wrath and fury soon will be unleashed upon a sinful humanity. Such soothsayers in politics, the media, or religion, even though their intentions may be honorable, have focused their attention far too prominently upon material—not spiritual—reality. They are pre–occupied with crime, drugs, poverty, the environment, and other *symptoms* of the true problem, our spiritual slumber.

Treating Causes, not Symptoms

Whenever we cultivate our spiritual nature, we lessen the true cause of our problems—*our spiritual slumber*. Once we have awakened, the symptoms will begin to vanish. As Thoreau and Holmes indicate, if we desire to reach our highest potential, then we must center our attention upon positive spiritual realities such as love, peace, joy, and harmony and not upon negative images such as destruction, judgment, and sin. We will achieve far greater success by creating positive images of ourselves living as enlightened beings in a divinely inspired universe than through creating negative images depicting our separation or isolation from God. The following suggestions nurture images of our true potential as infinite spiritual beings.

1. Affirm a positive future — Do not focus upon the horrors or judgments that could befall us or upon your own shortcomings in the past. Instead, focus upon our true spiritual potential that emanates from what Thoreau calls "our divine core." Activate the Unlimited Power of your Mind and join with others to create the future that God, the Universal Mind, intends for us as enlightened beings. Use affirmations such as the following to replace worry, anxiety, and doubt about the future. Focusing upon our shortcomings, and not upon our true spiritual nature, wastes the precious gift of unlimited human potential that God has given us.

- I am filled with a sense of peace and harmony about the future.
- I accept my role as part of a Spiritual Renaissance.
- I know the future contains harmony and peace.
- I feel my spiritual kinship with Nature.
- I am part of God's plan for a positive, harmonious future.
- I accept my true potential to be an enlightened child of God , the Universal Creative Essence.
- My life is a journey.

2. Act as if your every action influences the future

Immanuel Kant's Categorical Imperative stated:

> Act only on that maxim whereby you can at the same time will that your act should become a universal law.

Kant realized that if we truly desire to improve our future, then we must assume responsibility for its development by acting as if everything we do were worthy of becoming a universal law or principle. This awareness would cause us to reflect more upon our actions, thereby leading us towards more harmonious relationships with others and the universe. The Categorical Imperative, since it recognizes both the power of our minds and of our actions, can guide our efforts to create a positive future.

3. Understand our need for spiritual experience —

"We need spiritual experience, a first–hand knowledge of life and Reality...Spiritual experience is the result of realizing that Presence which binds all together in one complete Whole."

Ernest Holmes, *The Science of Mind*

"We must ask: have I any religious experience and immediate relation to God? To this question there is a positive answer only when the individual is willing to fulfill the demands of rigorous self–examination and self–knowledge."

Carl Jung, *The Undiscovered Self*

If we understand our genuine need for spiritual experience, then we may begin to awaken from our spiritual slumber. You may wish to complete the Spiritual Self–assessment that follows to gain more insight into what a spiritual experience of life entails by doing as Jung suggests—*self–examination*. Use the following ideas as a guide to list what you consider to be your present strengths and weaknesses for living a spiritual life. Use the results to inspire the journey ahead. It also is helpful to re–assess our spiritual experience of life periodically.

What is a Spiritual Experience of Life?

• Seeking wisdom from the essence of things, not from their surface or appearance; Truth comes from essence

- Seeking to create one's life with guidance from a source greater than one's ordinary consciousness; that source is the Universal Mind

- Not being influenced by the world's continually changing values

- Nonattachment to material or sensual pleasures

- Seeking to live a truly productive life employing one's talents to meet the needs of others

- Choosing to do those things or think those thoughts that contribute meaning to life and avoiding any thoughts or actions that do not

- Devoting as much time and energy to spiritual growth as to career, recreational, and family matters

- Developing one's "inner voice"—the Truth within—to the point we can distinguish it from one's "ego's voice"

- Actively working to find harmony and balance in life through meditation, dreamwork, creating an alliance with Nature, or spiritual counseling activities.

- Living in the eternal "now"

- Seeking to profit only from a "right livelihood" — from business activities that are honorable, meaningful, and do not harm others or Nature

- Loving others as we love ourselves

- Devotion to experiencing increasingly higher levels of spiritual involvement in one's life

"In proportion as a man simplifies his life, the laws of the universe will appear less complex."

Thoreau, *Walden*

"Thoreau cleared out of his life every custom and apparatus which could not stand up and justify its existence."

Lewis Mumford, *Images and Forecasts*

"We have made a riddle out of simplicity; therefore, we have not read the sermons written in stones, nor interpreted the light of love running through life."

Ernest Holmes, *The Science of Mind*

PREVIEW: Simplifying Our Lives

- **Discover Your "Complexities"**
- **Clear Out Mental Clutter**
- **Clear Out Physical Clutter**
- **Discover "True Economy"**
- **Applying Natural Principles**

The primary reason why we should simplify our lives—even by returning to less sophisticated ways of living if necessary—is that we are better able to clarify basic connections between ourselves and Nature. Nature is a web of intricate relationships that interact to produce harmony and balance. Thoreau, as well as Native Americans and contemporary spiritual leaders such as Ernest Holmes, realized that we can discern the spiritual wisdom expressed in Nature's relationships and use this wisdom to create harmony in our own lives. Unfortunately, modern society's complexity (true even in Thoreau's day) creates mental "clutter" which is a significant impediment to discerning the relationships responsible for Nature's harmony and balance.

If we reduce the mental clutter in our lives, the stress produced by attending to the clutter will diminish considerably. Once we reduce our mental clutter and the stress it generates, we can focus our awareness upon discovering the spiritual principles responsible for Nature's harmony and balance. When we understand these principles and experience for ourselves the natural harmony they produce, we begin to live more deliberately.

"What is my relationship with Nature?"

From Thoreau's perspective, self–realization is not as much discovering "Who am I?" as "What is my relationship with Nature?" Understanding this relationship enables us to know ourselves fully and truthfully. Full and truthful self–knowledge is the impetus for activating our highest potential. Throughout *Walden*, Thoreau makes it clear that realizing our highest potential begins by establishing an intimate relationship with Nature's simplicity, balance, and harmony—for in Nature, spiritual principles operate at all levels.

EXPERIMENT ONE:
DISCOVER YOUR "COMPLEXITIES"

"As for the complex ways of living, I love
them not, however much I practice them. In
as many places as possible, I will get my feet
down to the earth!"

Thoreau, *Journals*

"Let us approach things simply and quietly."

Ernest Holmes, *The Science of Mind*

1. Make a list of five things that you feel are complicating
your life—things that prevent your living more simply than
you feel you could live. These items could be material
objects, personal or business relationships, your negative
thoughts, societal issues, or anything else that you feel
thwarts your living more simply than you could.

2. Select one of the items as your first target for understanding your present complexities. Jot down all the
reasons you feel this particular item complicates your life
and prevents you from living more simply, more in
harmony with Nature's spiritual principles.

3. Next, list potential reasons why this item might be in
your life at the present moment. Is it there to meet an actual
need of yours? Did you *choose* to include this item in your
life, or is it there because you really have not focused your
awareness upon why it is there or what purpose it serves?
Explore what this could mean to you.

4. Once you have focused upon the potential purpose this "complexity" might serve, determine the steps you could take to simplify (or eliminate altogether if appropriate) this item in your life. List each activity that might be required to nurture simplicity in this area of your life. Implement these steps and observe the results. Record in your journal any insights that your efforts to remove complexities have provided you.

5. Repeat the process for the other four items on your list. Once you have created simplicity in these areas, create new lists and continue simplifying your life. Also, periodically review areas that you have simplified to discern if any complexities have returned.

EXPERIMENT TWO: CLEAR OUT MENTAL CLUTTER

"I believe that the mind can be permanently profaned by the habit of attending to the trivial."

Thoreau, *Life Without Principles*

"*Thoughts are Things!* Modern psychology affirms that all the thoughts and emotions we have experienced since we came into conscious existence are still present in the Mind, where ceaselessly active, they manifest themselves as subjective tendencies that mold the body in health or sickness; and determine, as well, our reactions to all life and experience."

Ernest Holmes, *The Science of Mind*

Do you continually repeat some thoughts to yourself? Do you experience thoughts that never seem to resolve themselves and just spontaneously "pop" into your mind? If you do, most likely these are your "cluttering thoughts" that will continue to engage your mind and prevent your living as simply and deliberately as is possible until you resolve them. Researchers indicate that experiencing cluttering thoughts has become prevalent in modern societies. Some people even have accepted them as an inevitable part of their lives.

As Thoreau and Holmes indicate, continuing to attend to these habitual cluttering thoughts profanes the mind and shapes our life experience *in the present.* If we desire to simplify our lives so we can live more deliberately, then we must replace these cluttering thoughts with new thoughts that can create possibilities for growth. First, determine which of the three types of cluttering thoughts seems to be most prevalent for you. Then, use the suggestions below to help remove these thoughts and to restore natural harmony and simplicity in your mental activities.

1. **Cluttering thoughts about the future:** If your cluttering thoughts are about your future and what you desire to happen, learn goal–setting techniques and relinquish your preoccupation with these thoughts once you have implemented goal–attainment strategies. Idle daydreaming about the future clutters the mind and saps our mental energy. Fully engaging yourself in life's activities NOW is the best way to ensure a desirable future. Refer to the exercises on daydreaming and meditation in the previous chapter for additional suggestions.

2. **Random cluttering thoughts**: If your cluttering thoughts appear to be random and do not seem to have any particular "theme," practice meditation and mindfulness exercises several times during the day—especially before

doing any activities where you have observed the presence of these random cluttering thoughts. Meditation and mindfulness exercises help create mental discipline and a more focused mind. When our mind becomes more focused, we are better able to discern our true relationship with Nature and to nurture simplicity.

3. **Self–image or Self–esteem Issues:** If your cluttering thoughts are about self–image or self–esteem issues—issues related to how you experienced yourself in the past, which, of course, shapes how you see yourself in the present—then learn techniques for dealing with these cluttering thoughts such as the one presented below. Pre-occupation with self–esteem issues, because it dwells upon the past and not your present life experience, will cloud your view of Nature and the principles for living deliberately. Also, you can use your meditation sessions to visualize and to affirm a more appropriate self–image.

Technique for Enhancing Self–image

Step One: Self–image Survey

1. On a blank piece of paper write down as many words or phrases as you can to describe yourself in the categories listed below. Include anything that you feel describes you. Continue to list items under a category heading until you feel you have exhausted that category.

A. Physical appearance	F. Job performance
B. Interpersonal relationships	G. Personality
C. Performing daily tasks of life	H. Mental functioning
D. How other people see you	I. Hobbies or interests
E. Intimate relationships	J. Creativity

2. Once you have written descriptions under the various headings, go back and place a plus (+) by items that you feel represent strengths or things you like about yourself. Put a minus (–) by the things you consider to be weaknesses or you do not like about yourself. If you consider an item to be simply an objective or neutral self–description, then do not mark it.

Step Two: Revising "Weaknesses"

1. Divide a blank sheet of paper into two equal columns. At the top of the left column, write the words "PRESENT SELF–IMAGE." Under this heading, list all the items marked with an minus from the inventory above. Leave several blank lines under each item as you will modify or rewrite each of these items in the column on the right.

2. Write the words "REVISED SELF–IMAGE" at the top of the right hand column. In this column you will rewrite each of the items you listed under the left column using the three guidelines listed below. You may need two or three statements for each revision.

Guidelines—Avoid Self–condemnation:

• Use language that is not belittling or derogatory. Avoid words such as *stupid, ugly, lousy, arrogant, fat,* etc. These words are **inherently negative**, and we must avoid these terms in self–descriptions.

• Use specific language and avoid overgeneralizations. Avoid terms such as *always, never, totally, every,* etc. as these indicate overgeneralizations. (*e.g.,* "I'm *always* forgetting things or I *never* remember people's names.") Overgeneralizing about ourselves obscures the truth from us which will prevent our living more deliberately. Cite *specific* instances or occasions rather than generalizations. For example, if you were rewriting the weakness "forgetful," you might write: "I tend to forget relative's birthdays" or "I forget to renew my safe deposit box." Be as factual and specific as possible when writing your revised list.

• Find exceptions to the weakness if you can. If you wrote "forgetful" as a weakness and can think of things about which you are not forgetful, then include these.

Step Three: Self–reflection and Feedback

1. Once you have rewritten each of the items under the "PRESENT SELF–IMAGE" list, it is time to reflect upon your new self–description. Read aloud each item from the left column, and then read aloud the revised version of it. Read the revised version with strong feeling, as if you were convincing yourself or others of it. Continue reading each item aloud in this manner until you have completed the entire list.

2. When you are through, write down your immediate thoughts, impressions, or feelings. What do you notice? What have you learned about yourself? How can you incorporate this awareness into your life activities? At least once a week for the next few weeks, read the list aloud and write down your observations. You also could do this anytime you feel down on yourself. Periodically, complete a "self–esteem" inventory and note any changes that occur.

Step Four: Integrating Your Insights into Life

1. Your self-reflection experience in the above step, most likely, will provide you with enhanced awareness of your cluttering self–image thoughts. Regularly practicing self–

refection will help you integrate your enhanced awareness
into the fabric of your life.

2. Anytime you find yourself cluttering your mind with
items from the unrevised list, immediately say to yourself:
"I'm using a cluttering thought. I have a *choice* about how
I express myself on this matter, and I *choose...* (use one
of the revised statements that would be appropriate for the
matter at hand)." In time, most likely, you will notice that
your self–image thoughts will gravitate naturally to the
those on the revised list. You will be replacing cluttering
thoughts that offer little or no potential for growth with
more empowering ones that create possibilities for growth.

EXPERIMENT THREE:
CLEAR OUT PHYSICAL CLUTTER

> "I buy but few things, and those not till long
> after I begin to want them, so that when I do
> get them I am prepared to make a perfect use
> of them."
>
> Thoreau, *Journals*

Have you ever said to yourself as you surveyed your
closets, attic, garage, storage rooms, or even your living
areas: "How in the world did I ever accumulate all this
stuff?" Most likely, each of us has asked ourselves this
question at some point. Unfortunately, most of us never
bother to answer the question, and herein lies our problem.
We often accumulate material items *mindlessly*. Little by
little, we acquire new things that "we can't live without" or
"we simply must have." We also may justify keeping an item
that has little use to us by invoking the nebulous "someday I
may need it" rationale. Giving ourselves these and similar

rationalizations seems to placate our mind and to justify acquiring yet another material object or to justify keeping objects that no longer serve a useful purpose. Through time, however, these material objects may become a source of complexity in our lives—even if they are secreted away in the closet or garage—because cluttering our physical environment with nonessential items can compound our mental clutter.

One group of Native Americans have an interesting ritual for dealing with accumulated material objects. Once in every generation, tribe members hold a ceremony in which they burn all their material possessions. This would assure that they would not accumulate unnecessary material items or that they would not become too attached to their material possessions. While you may not be willing to use their ceremonial manner for dealing with the problem of accumulated materials objects, you can employ the *principle* behind their method. The following suggestion will help you become more mindful of your tendency to acquire material items, especially ones that end up as "stuff."

Initial Consideration: "Waste" vs. "Trash"

One of modern society's greatest misunderstandings is its apparent confusion between the words "waste" and "trash." Most people use these terms interchangeably, and this creates two unhealthy realities: it prevents our living more deliberately, and it creates a violent assault upon Nature. Learning to distinguish between these words is an essential component of applying spiritual principles in life.

Waste refers to something that has no use or value to the person to whom it belongs; however, it does possess value to other people or in other applications. *Waste should be recycled.*

Trash, on the other hand, refers to something that has no use or value to anyone. Trash should be discarded *properly*.

Aluminum products, glass products, newspapers, food scraps, yard wastes, most paper and plastic products, repairable objects, and many other commonly "trashed" items are actually waste. Proper disposal of these items occurs only through recycling or repairing— *not through any other means*. If confusion of waste with trash has prevented you from recycling waste, you need only to change your perception about what you put into your garbage cans or haul to the dump. Changing your perception so that you distinguish waste from trash will be a significant step towards living more deliberately and saving Nature from our indifference. A suggestion to accomplish this goal follows:

Have separate containers for waste and trash to facilitate recycling and to develop "waste–consciousness." As a preliminary way to raise "waste–consciousness," **do not put anything into the trash container until you have asked yourself these questions:**

- Can this be of use to other people or in other applications? Use your imagination!

- Can this be recycled? (glass, aluminum, many plastics, paper, etc.)

- Can this be composted? (food scraps, grass, leaves, twigs, etc.)

- Can this be repaired?

Physical Clutter Survey

1. Rummage through your closets, garage, living areas, office, attic, etc. and list any particular items that you consider to be physical "clutter." For our purpose, clutter may include items such as:

- items needing to be repaired
- items that are broken "beyond repair"
- items that you feel are no longer in "style"
- items belonging to other people, but are in your possession for any reason
- items that you intend to give to charities
- items that will be useful "someday"
- items of "sentimental value"
- items that should be in more appropriate storage facilities
- items that are duplicates or essentially the same as other of your possessions

2. Once you have made your list, jot down the reasons why *each particular item* is on your list using the ideas in the step above. Do you notice any "theme" emerging about your physical clutter. For example, if you had many items that were duplicates of other items or were no longer in "style," consider the implications of these observations. Write down any insights you have received about the nature of your present physical clutter and the potential implications of continuing to have it in your possession. Consider what produces your tendency to generate physical clutter in your environment. Complete this survey periodically to monitor your physical clutter.

Eliminating Physical Clutter

NOTE: The purpose of the following exercise is to help us become mindful of how and why we tend to clutter our environment before we discard unnecessary physical clutter. Simply hauling everything away without gaining insight into why we clutter inevitably will lead us back to a cluttered environment. Also, this exercise depends upon your having completed the preceding exercise.

1. Select one area of your environment (a closet, garage, attic, your desk, etc.) that you feel is cluttered to the extent that it occasionally bothers you.

2. Choose one of the characteristics of "clutter" (e.g., items needing repair, items of sentimental value, etc.) listed in the preceding exercise. This will be your target for now.

3. Collect all items that fit into this category and place them in front of you. Spend a moment thinking about each item in light of the questions below. You may wish to write down your responses.

- What is my immediate reaction to this item?
- What was my original purpose or reason for acquiring it?
- Why is it now "clutter?"
- Why do I keep it around?
- Does it have a useful purpose either to me or other people at this time?
- Would I ever need to acquire another one of these?
- What have I learned from thinking about this object?

4. ACT! Use the insights gleaned from your observations to help you clear out clutter from this environment. Do whatever is appropriate for each item (trash, repair, return, sell, transform into something useful, etc.) Once you have cleared out items in your chosen category, proceed to the other categories. Once you have cleared out any particular environment, move on to others that you feel are cluttered.

EXPERIMENT FOUR: PROVIDE FOR YOURSELF WITH "TRUE ECONOMY"

> "Who knows, but if men constructed their dwellings for themselves with their own hands, and provided food for themselves and their families simply and honestly enough, the poetic quality would be universally developed, as birds universally sing when they are so engaged?"
>
> Thoreau, *Walden*

> "I have done without electricity and tend the fireplace and stove myself. Evenings, I light the old lamps. There is no running water, and I pump the water from the well. I chop wood and cook the food. These simple acts make man simple...I live in modest harmony with nature."
>
> Carl Jung, *Memories, Dreams, Reflections*

One of the most crucial elements of living deliberately is that we must be able to distinguish between things that are necessities of life and things that are luxuries. In *Walden*, Thoreau presents a consequence of the inability to distinguish between necessities and luxuries:

> Men have come to such a pass that they frequently starve, not for the want of necessities, but for want of luxuries.

Thoreau feels that our obsession with materialistic pleasures has blurred the line between *necessity* and *luxury* to such an extent that we may feel miserable when luxuries—not just necessities—are difficult to obtain. In other words, luxuries have become necessities to us, and we can suffer whenever we are without a luxury "fix." If we are sincere about living more simply in order to discern Nature's spiritual principles, then we must learn to distinguish between necessities and luxuries. Thoreau will be our guide.

Distinguishing *Necessities* from *Luxuries*

Thoreau makes clear his idea of life's necessities quite early in *Walden*:

> By the words, necessity of life, I mean whatever, of all that man obtains by his own exertions has been from the first, or from long use has become, so important to human life that few, if any, whether from savageness, or poverty, or philosophy, ever attempt to do without it.

Necessities, therefore, are those things which directly support the continuance of life as evidenced by our historical requirement of their availability. Necessities make life possible, not make it more stylish, comfortable, or convenient. Thoreau classifies necessities into four basic areas: food, clothing, shelter, and fuel. Readers who are familiar with Buddha's teaching may notice a striking parallel between Thoreau's definition of necessities and that of Buddha who felt necessities to be food, clothing, shelter, and health care. The similarity between an ancient Eastern and a modern Western perspective should give us a strong indication of what actually constitutes a necessity—*items that are required for human survival*. With this in mind, let's turn to Thoreau's ideas about luxuries.

Luxuries, according to Thoreau, are items that are not necessary for our survival—*they are items which make life more convenient or fashionable*. First, luxuries embody the principle of making our life easier or our tasks more convenient. Nothing comes without a price, however, and the price that both we and Nature pay for convenience items (e.g. "scrubbing bubbles," microwave ovens and foods, plastic, disposable diapers, *ad infinitum*) is unconscionable. Our attachment to convenience not only endangers the environment, but it also gives us the illusion that we are simplifying our lives. **Convenience is counterfeit simplicity**. It is impossible to simplify our lives and to live more deliberately if we harm Nature in the process. To the extent that we transcend the desire for convenience, we will have taken a giant step towards living more deliberately and saving the planet from the consequences of our addiction to counterfeit simplicity.

A second characteristic of luxuries embodies the principle of **ego-involvement** in the purchasing decision. For example, if we make purchasing decisions based upon fashion or style considerations, then what are our real intentions for acquiring the item? Fashion or style considerations reflect ego–needs, our attachment to something other than the item's usefulness to meeting our true needs. Certainly we need items such as sweaters to keep us warm in winter; however, if our primary motivation for choosing among various sweaters is to buy one with a designer label or to buy whatever is currently chic, then we are paying homage to our ego needs—not our true need, which is simply to keep warm in winter.

Another inherent drawback to stylistic considerations is that whenever we purchase an item primarily for style or fashion purposes, its usefulness to us is tempered by the reality that as soon as it is no longer stylish—regardless of its condition or suitability for further use—then we must replace the item with "the latest style." Fashion or style considerations, since they are directed at meeting nonessential ego–needs—not our survival needs—direct us away from living more deliberately. To the extent that we transcend the need to be stylish, we will have taken a giant step towards simplifying our lives and living in harmony with Nature. We also will have prepared ourselves to understand the principle of "true economy."

```
┌──────────────────────────────────────────┐
│              REMEMBER:                   │
│  • Necessities make life possible.       │
│  • Luxuries make life convenient or stylish. │
└──────────────────────────────────────────┘
```

Understanding "True Economy"

Once we have learned to distinguish between what is truly necessary in our lives and what is merely a convenience or an ego–gratifying style consideration, Thoreau feels that we can live according to the principle of "true economy." In true economy, we are directly involved *as much as possible* in providing our necessities: we grow our food, bake our bread, mend and sew our clothing, build and repair our houses and furniture, repair our possessions, etc. Being directly involved with providing our own necessities creates a sense of purpose and joy in our lives that we would otherwise miss if we depended upon others to provide these necessities for us.

If we are divorced from personally providing for our basic needs, Thoreau tells us we are involved with a "false economy," because we work to acquire the means of having others provide our food, clothing, and other necessities for us. If we live by the principle of "false economy," then we may experience a distorted or "false" sense of purpose in life, and we will not be living deliberately.

The more directly involved we are in the process of providing our necessities, the more joy and satisfaction we will experience in all our activities. Granted, our modern surroundings may preclude *full* participation in this process; however, in proportion as we provide our basic necessities by using our own hands, the greater the joy we will experience with this life requirement. As Carl Jung notes above, even performing simple tasks will bring great joy and will help us to live more deliberately. Our first step towards the more deliberate lifestyle that Jung and Thoreau describe in their thoughts above is learning how to differentiate between necessities and luxuries. The activities below facilitate this objective. Later, you will find activities that will help you develop "true economy."

PART ONE: Activities to Distinguish between Necessities and Luxuries

A Personal Definition of "Necessities" and "Luxuries"

1. Take a blank sheet of paper and draw a line down the center to form two columns. At the top of the left hand column, write "Necessities" and on the right, "Luxuries."

2. In the "Necessities" column, list whatever you feel are the characteristics of something that is a necessity to you. Leave a small blank space after each characteristic you list and continue on another sheet of paper, if necessary. Be as honest, sincere, and thorough as possible as you create your list. Remember, these will be your own perceptions about necessities.

3. Create a similar list of your thoughts about luxuries in the "Luxuries" column.

4. Write down your immediate thoughts and impressions after completing these preliminary steps. Do you have any new insights about how to distinguish between necessities and luxuries? Have any new questions or issues arisen?

5. Next, select one of the characteristics of "Necessities." Take a tour of your home and find a few items that will meet this characteristic. Write these items in the blank space beneath the characteristic. Continue until you have identified a few items to meet each of the characteristics of "Necessities." Once you finish your hunt for "Necessities," then repeat the process for "Luxuries."

6. Now it is time to reflect upon your activities. Write down any thoughts or observations that you have at this time. If you desire a few suggestions, consider the following:

- What have I learned about how I distinguish between a necessity and a luxury?

- What type of items (clothing, food items, books, appliances, etc.) did I find it easiest to distinguish between necessities and luxuries? The most difficult? What does this tell me?

- What characteristics of either "Necessities" or "Luxuries" would I now revise? How would I revise them? Why?

- What is the role of my ego in determining the difference between a necessity and a luxury? In which type of item (clothing, food items, books, appliances, etc.) was my ego the least involved? The most? What does this tell me?

- In the future, how can I apply what I have observed by doing this activity to my goal of living more deliberately?

7. Finally, write a definition in your own words for "necessity" and "luxury," using the insights gained from this experience. Use your definitions when making purchasing decisions in the future to determine if a prospective purchase is really a necessity or a luxury. Periodically, redefine these two terms to reflect any new insights you have gathered from your life journey.

- **To me, a necessity is:**

- **To me, a luxury is:**

The Purchase Survey Activity

1. Make a list of the purchases you made in the past week (or the past day or two if you have made many purchases). Include as many items as possible that you have purchased, even if they seem trivial or small. If you went grocery shopping or otherwise purchased a large assortment of items, list as many of the individual items as you can remember. Also, consider paying a bill (utility, charge card, insurance, etc.) as making a purchase.

2. Take a blank sheet of paper and divide it into 4 columns: **Food, Clothing, Shelter,** and **Fuel & Health Care** (note these four categories reflect Thoreau's and Buddha's definitions of necessities). Next, place items from the list in step one in their appropriate column. If you feel an item does not fit in any of these 4 columns, omit it for now.

3. Once you have placed items in their appropriate columns, begin with the first item in the food column. Consider for a moment your purchase of that particular item. Reflect upon considerations such as:

- Is this item truly necessary to sustain my life? Why or why not?

- Were there alternatives to buying this particular item (buying a different brand, buying a less or more expensive variety of this item, buying sale items, buying a different product to meet this need, etc.)? If so, why did I reject the alternatives and purchase this item?

- Did I have any "convenience" considerations in mind as I made this purchase? If so, what were they? At what "price" did I obtain this counterfeit simplicity?

- Were there any ego–involvement considerations (*i.e.*, style or fashion considerations) in this purchase? If so, what were they? How did these affect my choice?

- What difference would it have made to my life if I had not bought this item at all?

4. Once you have given the item active consideration, determine if you made this purchase based upon it being more of a necessity or a luxury. Use whatever is your current understanding of these two terms as your guide. Mark each item with a "N" for necessity or a "L" for luxury to reflect its appropriate purchase consideration.

5. Continue evaluating your purchase of the other items on the list. When you have finished, write down your immediate impressions of your purchasing decisions. What have you noticed about your ability to distinguish between necessities and luxuries? Would there be any changes that you now would like to make? In which of the four categories was it easiest to distinguish between purchasing out of necessity versus out of luxury considerations? In which was it most difficult? With these new insights in mind, determine what can you do in the future to live more deliberately.

6. Periodically perform other purchase surveys to heighten your awareness of your ability to make purchases that help you live more deliberately.

7. "Other Items"—For any items on your list that you feel did not fall into any of the 4 categories that Thoreau considers to be necessities, determine if *you* feel it is a necessity. Consider what makes it a necessity for you and why. Jot down your thoughts and impressions.

Mindful Shopping Activity

The next time you go shopping (grocery shopping will work especially well), use the following suggestions to help you shop more mindfully. Before you select any item, reflect upon the following ideas:

• What is my primary reason for buying this item?

• Am I making this purchase with "convenience" in mind (i.e., the item is designed to save time or effort: microwave foods, frozen precooked items, cake mixes, packaged meals, or anything else with "convenience" as part of its essential nature)?

• Do I have any ego–involvement with this item (i.e., style or fashion considerations or any other considerations such as it being a "gourmet" item or considerations for how others may think or feel about this item)?

• Does advertising affect my purchasing decision in any way? If so, how and why? What does this tell me?

• Are there any alternatives to buying this item that would help me live more deliberately?

The Mindful "Major" Purchase Activity

The next time you have to make a "major" purchase (suggestions for determining this include: clothing, appliances, dining out, travel, or any item above a certain pre–determined dollar amount), use the guidelines in the exercise above to help you make a purchasing decision that reflects your attempt to live more deliberately.

PART TWO: Activities to Promote Living by "True Economy"

We promote "true economy" when we:

* grow as much of our own food (hopefully, by organic methods!) as possible—if you have no experience, start with a few easy–to–grow vegetables and herbs (tomatoes, peppers, basil, chives, and oregano, for example) and increase the garden size and content as you gain experience

* can, freeze, or preserve our own food—from either our garden or from sources such as co–ops/farmers markets

* develop a compost pile to turn food scraps, leaves, and grass clippings into fertilizer for next year's food crop

* cook as much as possible without using pre–cooked items, frozen entrées, mixes of any kind, or other "pseudo–conveniences"

* bake as much of our own bread as possible

* make our own yogurt, cheese, beer, and wine

* do as much of our own household labor as possible (repairs, yard work, painting, ironing, cleaning, etc.)

* avoid purchasing anything "disposable"

* buy products in sturdy packaging such as glass jars that we can use as storage containers

* make gifts for other people instead of buying gifts

* make greeting and holiday cards ourselves

- switch from modern "convenience" cleansers (highly toxic to us, our children and pets, and Nature!) to safer, more natural cleansers such as bio–degradable soap, baking soda, borax, lemon juice, etc.

- *as much as reasonably possible*, avoid "agents" (people whose actions prevent our handling certain tasks ourselves: doctors, accountants, lawyers, therapists, real estate agents, and other "experts," etc.)—we must assume responsibility for our own lives and well–being; we can learn what must be done and **do it ourselves!**

Periodically, write down your thoughts and impressions about doing the above elements of "true economy." Observe the following and other considerations:

- how you feel while you perform the activity

- how you feel as you enjoy the fruits of your labor

- your overall mental, spiritual, and physical "wellness"

- your effect upon others by these efforts

- your effect upon Nature

- what you have learned by performing these activities in the spirit of "true economy"

EXPERIMENT FIVE: APPLYING NATURAL PRINCIPLES

"How important is a constant intercourse with nature and the contemplation of natural phenomena to the preservation of moral and intellectual health!"

Thoreau, *Journals*

"This we know—all things are connected,
like the blood that unites a family. All things
are connected."

Chief Seattle, chief of the Suquamish People

Once we begin to clear out mental and physical clutter, to distinguish between necessities and luxuries, and to provide for ourselves with the principle of true economy, then, most likely, we will have simplified our lives to the point that we can discern the remarkable harmony and balance that permeates Nature. The interrelationship among Nature's various systems creates *synergy*, a spiritual principle that manifests itself in Nature. Even apparently "destructive" forces such as forest fires, tornadoes, earthquakes, hurricanes, or volcanoes are a part of Nature's synergism, which eventually will benefit the whole system.

Nature's harmony and balance are spiritual principles; they are divine realities manifest in physical form. These principles, therefore, could teach humanity invaluable lessons that would help us harmonize and balance our lives. The major stumbling block to our leading a more concordant life has been our pre–occupation with solving "human" problems: disease, poverty, drugs, war, injustice, infidelity, hostility, etc. These are not our real problems. They are merely symptoms of our overly complex lifestyle in which we have divorced ourselves from Nature. Our problem is that we have not learned to draw upon Nature's harmony and balance (a divine reality) as a guide for our lives.

Once we have simplified our lives sufficiently to discern Nature's basic relationships and the spiritual principles responsible for these relationships, we can use this wisdom to create harmony and balance in our lives. We must not forget that we are part of Nature. Nor should we forget that our lives can operate as part of Nature. Listed below are several examples of Nature's relationships and how they can apply in human affairs. Whenever you feel the need for guidance with a problem or decision that you must make, select one of these natural relationships and look for ways you can apply it to your present situation. Through time, you may discover other relationships that offer guidance for living more deliberately.

Natural Principles and Their Significance to Us

Natural Principle---------- Wholeness & Unity

• Examples from Nature

Virtually all plants and animals are individual, self–contained life units, but each individual life unit has a relationship with and a value to the whole; all life is interrelated

• Significance to Us

We can experience ourselves both as an individual and as part of all life; we can feel less isolated from each other and from Nature; we can feel ourselves to be less a "victim of circumstances beyond our control"

Natural Principle---------- Symbiosis

• Examples from Nature

Lichen—the fungus part of lichen provides the algae part with a place to live, and the algae part furnishes food for the fungus, which is a parasite and cannot provide its own food

Plants breathe carbon dioxide exhaled by animals and transform it into oxygen that animals breathe

- ## Significance to Us

Humans can cooperate both with each other and with other lifeforms to create "win–win" opportunities in all our activities

Natural Principle---------- Sustainability

- ## Examples from Nature

Most animals consume only the food necessary to sustain their own lives; they do not endanger their own or other lifeforms' future by over–consuming

- ## Significance to Us

Humans can learn that the future of all life requires that we live wisely *now*; we must cultivate and use sustainable technologies and live more simply *now*

Natural Principle---------- Flexibility

- ## Examples from Nature

Trees and other plants blow in the wind or bend downwards during a rainstorm to avoid damage

Most animals will abandon their customary or preferred food during times of scarcity and will eat what is plentiful

- ## Significance to Us

We often become rigid and set in our ways as we age; we must maintain flexibility in all our encounters; flexing our "mental muscles" is healthy, just as is flexing our physical muscles

Natural Principle---------- Life Rhythms

- ## Examples from Nature

Seasons, heartbeats, mating periods, moon cycles, menstruation, planting and harvesting, tides, etc.

• Significance to Us

We can learn that life has many ebbs and flows; we can learn to endure life's natural peaks and valleys; we can learn to live in harmony with the natural rhythms around us; "to everything, there is a season"

NOTE: The ideas above are suggestions to help you get started in applying natural principles to your needs. Spend time in Nature discerning other principles that you can apply in your life activities. Nature is a treasure–trove of spiritual wisdom waiting to help us live more deliberately.

EXPERIMENTS IN RE-ALLYING WITH NATURE

"We must go out and re–ally ourselves with nature every day."

Thoreau, *Walden*

The Earth, her life am I.
The Earth, her body is my body.
The Earth, her thoughts are my
  thoughts.

Navajo Chant

PREVIEW: Re–allying with Nature

- **Observe the Three Laws of Ecology**
- **Present–Tense Awareness**
- **Liberate Your Perception**
- **Expand Awareness of Nature through Sound, Smell, and Touch**
- **Nurture Synesthetic Awareness**
- **Verbalize Out Loud While in Nature**
- **Let Native American Ideas Guide You**

Have you ever speculated whether a connection exists between humanity's disregard for Mother Earth and the tension and stress that is so characteristic of modern humanity. Perhaps you—like Thoreau in his use of the term "re–ally" in the quotation opening this chapter—also have speculated that humanity at one time actually experienced an intimate alliance with Nature and her spiritual energies. Several penetrating questions could emerge from these and similar speculations: "Are there definitive benefits of our being intimately allied with Nature?," "What caused us to turn away from our alliance with Nature?," and "How do we re–ally ourselves with Nature?" This chapter addresses each of these questions. We begin by exploring the potential benefits we would receive through a personal alliance with Nature.

Thoreau's Ideas: Benefits of an Alliance with Nature

> "When I hear a robin sing at sunset, I cannot help contrasting the equanimity of Nature with the bustle and impatience of man."

> "Nature, even when she is scant and thin outwardly, contents us still by the assurance of a certain generosity at the roots."

> "I see, smell, taste, hear, feel that everlasting Something to which we are all allied, our Maker, our abode, our destiny, our very selves."

> Thoreau, *Journals*

Thoreau suggests that the potential benefits of an intimate alliance between ourselves and Nature may have psychological as well as environmental implications. His speculations have been confirmed by many modern psychologists who note that contemporary society's predominant mindset displays considerable tension and stress. We compound this tension by our feelings of isolation from each other and from Nature's spiritual energies. As long as we experience ourselves as isolated from each other and Nature, we may develop feelings of personal inadequacy—even if we are "successful" by society's standards. Money, fame, power, and material possessions cannot substitute for the spiritual contentment we can receive from an intimate alliance with Nature. Attending to these material concerns diverts us away from the spiritual energies found in Nature and creates the tension and stress prevalent in modern humanity, tension that we ultimately channel back into the environment.

Consider for a moment the following potential benefits of creating an intimate alliance with Nature's spiritual energies. Reflect upon the degree that you presently experience each benefit in your life. If there are other benefits that you feel may emanate from an alliance with Nature, please add them to the list. Keep these benefits in mind as you use the activities for re–allying yourself with Nature. In addition, refer to the exercise "Applying Natural Relationships" presented in the previous chapter.

Potential Benefits of an Alliance with Nature

- Enhanced spiritual awareness, a sense of unity with Nature and the spiritual reality that underlies Nature

- Less tension and stress, greater satisfaction with life "just as it is" without anxiety over how it "should be"

- Less reliance upon material pleasures as a means of determining our self–worth

- Greater sense of purpose in life; a sense that everything we do is significant; everything affects the Whole

- Feelings of harmony and balance similar to Nature's harmony and balance

- Greater appreciation for Nature as a physical manifestation of Spiritual Principles

- Fewer feelings of isolation from others or from Nature

- Greater awareness of our role in maintaining Nature's beauty and harmony

At Home, in the "Garden of Eden"

Many people we might label "primitive" (both historic and contemporary) experience a profound spiritual alliance between themselves and Nature that enables them to survive without injuring or destroying the web of life, of which they feel themselves to be an integral part. Because they respect *all life* as part of the "Great Spirit" that resides within Nature, they consume the planet's resources in a manner that maintains natural harmony and balance. Today, as in the past, hunting tribes kill only when necessary to provide food, not for sport or animal "trophies" to hang on the wall. Their rituals and ceremonies pay homage to the spirit of each animal they kill to provide food. They also make constructive use of every part of its body. Likewise, planting tribes respect Mother Earth's natural cycles and pay respect to her by tilling only enough ground to provide food. "Primitive" people, because they feel themselves to be in an alliance with Nature, have lived for many thousands of years without causing as much destruction of Nature as have "civilized" people (*i.e.* European or Western cultures) during the past decade.

To understand the deep roots beneath Western civilization's march away from our former alliance with Nature, we can turn to the early seventeenth century and the works of Francis Bacon. In 1620, Bacon published an earth–shattering book, *Novum Organum*. His book challenged the long–standing Socratic/Platonic/Aristotelian method of scientific inquiry with its emphasis upon understanding the unseen Spiritual or "Ideal" Reality responsible for what we perceive as physical reality. Discovering the unseen principles (the Transcendent) behind the surface of reality brought humanity enlightenment and a sense of participation in the Universal Plan. We experienced ourselves to be an integral part of Nature. Bacon's book, however, sought principles to make human life easier —*even if it meant unraveling our connections with Nature.* Human convenience had replaced spiritual enlightenment as the prime motivation for scientific inquiry.

Kicked Out of the Garden

Bacon's methodology was purely materialistic, because he advocated a total separation of spirit from matter. It emphasized that we must divorce ourselves completely from Nature if we are to be proper observers of natural phenomenon. Bacon claimed that humanity must no longer see itself as part of Nature as we had done since ancient Greece, for this would unnecessarily prejudice our scientific observations. Once freed of the "blinders" of seeing ourselves as part of Nature, we could marshal our energies into developing the most efficient methods to conquer Nature in order to advance humanity's materialistic ends. Bacon summarized his arguments for a new direction in scientific inquiry with this statement: "The goal of scientific study is to enlarge the bounds of human empire." Nature was now our slave, not our intimate friend and ally.

Our exploration into the roots of our separation from Nature does not end with Bacon. His transformation of the Earth into an easily manipulated hulk opened the door for other materialistic thinkers such as Adam Smith and John Locke. Smith, also blind to spirit, built upon Bacon's premise that the Earth is an exploitable mass. He claimed that humanity's material self–interest was the primary motivating force behind all human activities and that each person increases the common good by exercising his or her own material self–interest. In other words, the more we seek material satisfaction as an individual, the more we could satisfy it as a society. Bacon merely enslaved Nature. Smith, on the other hand, provided us with a "socially redeeming" motivation for exploiting Mother Earth's natural resources and for further distancing ourselves from Nature.

While Bacon had separated us from Nature and Smith had given us material self–interest, it took John Locke to nail the coffin shut on humanity's unity with Nature. Locke's contribution to this drama was the conception that unending material progress was not only humanity's birthright, but also its "salvation." He championed continual exploitation of natural resources, because he felt that "land that is left wholly to nature...is called, as indeed it is, waste." To Locke, Nature was an unproductive and undeveloped *wasteland* that humanity must transform into an Earthly Eden. The Industrial Revolution soon followed, and the blueprint that Bacon, Smith, and Locke had drawn for humanity's relationship with Nature became the foundation for both our present isolation from Nature and the incumbent environmental destruction.

Material Blindness

Today, as a result of "human progress," we stand at the threshold of eliminating not only our own lifeform from this planet, but also virtually all lifeforms around us as well. Through our unrelenting assault upon the planet's resources, we already have eliminated countless species from the biosphere, destroyed millions of acres of natural forests, overgrazed pasture lands to feed our addiction to eating animal flesh, clogged the atmosphere, poisoned the waterways, and have saturated the landscape with landfills that are bursting at the seams. Yet, in spite of these clear and present dangers, our media continue to bombard us with the message that "to consume is to enjoy life, to be a part of the American Dream." Our isolation from Nature and our incessant drive for materialistic pleasures have put all life on Earth on the brink of extinction, something that materialistically oriented thinkers such as Bacon, Smith, and Locke apparently could not foresee.

One reason they could not predict the planet's impending demise comes from a fundamental fallacy in their thinking— their notion that matter and spirit are separate, or, in other words, that we and Nature are separate. Disregarding our connection to the spiritual presence within Nature has created an anthropocentric mindset. By believing that *all* human needs can be harvested from Nature, we have created an enormous spiritual "void" in ourselves, a void that must be filled with *something* if we are to feel satisfied with life. Unfortunately, materialistic pleasures cannot satisfy spiritual hunger; therefore, in spite of feeding ourselves increasingly larger doses of material pleasures, our spiritual nature cries out for nurturing.

Because many people today are fairly unfamiliar with their spiritual connection with Nature, they inevitably turn to the only source of satisfaction with which they are familiar— materialistic pleasures—in a futile effort to satiate their inner spiritual hunger. A vicious cycle then exists, and the craving for materialistic pleasures as a means to appease spiritual hunger produces devastating results. For the individual, this cycle can produce tension, stress, and an overall dissatisfaction with life. For the environment, it can create an assault upon Nature's resources to satisfy our true spiritual hunger with material resources. Since Nature's resources are fragile—*and we are spiritually malnourished*—we must break this cycle if we and Nature are to survive.

Consider these thoughts for a few minutes

"The only way out is spiritual, intellectual, and emotional revolution in which, finally, we learn to experience first–hand the interlooping connections between person and person, organism and organism, action and consequence."

Gregory Bateson

"The survival of Earth depends upon 're-inventing our species' so that we live more harmoniously with Nature. The new cosmology that science, art, and mysticism unite to teach is the ancient spiritual and ecological lesson: all things are connected."

Matthew Fox, *My Final Statement before being Silenced by the Vatican*

Do you feel that Thoreau would agree with these modern thinkers? Would he feel that a re–alliance with Nature is a form of "re–inventing" our species? Would you be willing to participate in the new cosmology or mindset that sees all things as being interconnected? Would you risk your attachment to your present lifestyle to obtain one that is more allied with the spiritual presence in Nature, one that creates balance and harmony in all that you do? If so, let's explore several activities for initiating this "spiritual renaissance."

EXPERIMENT ONE: LEARN AND OBSERVE THE THREE LAWS OF ECOLOGY

"How is it that man always feels like an interloper in Nature, as if he had intruded on the domains of the bird and beast."

Thoreau, *Journals*

THE THREE LAWS OF ECOLOGY

First Law: All forms of life are interdependent and interrelated. When one is disturbed or harmed, *all are disturbed or harmed.*

Second Law: The stability of ecosystems is dependent upon their diversity. Greater diversity means more stability. Eliminating some lifeforms reduces stability of the whole ecosphere.

Third Law: We must conserve natural resources.

(adapted from Patrick Moore, co-founder of Greenpeace)

Ecology can be applied at the most minute, personal levels of behavior as well as at the largest, most cosmic levels. Observe, as did Thoreau, how you interact with the natural ecological systems around you. Pay attention to your interactions with Nature as you walk, camp, hike, or conduct your ordinary daily activities. Determine if you are intruding in any area and cease that practice immediately. Learn to experience Nature as yourself. Once we see that we and Nature are one, we are more likely to re–ally ourselves with Nature. We will walk in Nature as a friend, not as an intruder.

> **NOTE:** Please be careful not to disturb Nature when conducting the following exercises. Do not remove from its location anything that would be harmed by such action. Remember, we want to be friends of Nature, not interlopers.

EXPERIMENT TWO: ENHANCE PRESENT–TENSE AWARENESS

"Now or never! You must live in the present, launch yourself on every wave, find eternity in each moment."

Thoreau, *Journals*

Ralph Waldo Emerson wrote that his friend Henry Thoreau's greatest strength was his ability to consume each moment of the day as if it were an exquisite delicacy. To Thoreau, the present moment was an eternity in which he could explore his relationships with Nature and live unencumbered by the preoccupation with the past or the future. Thoreau was not alone in his love for the present moment. Vincent van Gogh strongly believed that losing oneself in the present and being inspired by Nature enhances our creative potential. Complete absorption in a natural object creates an "encounter" that helps us overcome routine, stereotypical thinking about whatever lies before us. We can use these encounters as a vital part of our efforts to re–ally ourselves with Nature.

Complete absorption in the present moment also was an important factor in Richard Wagner's creative inspiration. He believed that present–tense awareness provided him with "a capacity to saturate all my being unreservedly with my subject which—protected thusly from trivial pursuits— grows in depth and intensity." His insight tells us why we must remain in the present, *to avoid trivial distractions.* Any form of distraction, especially our thoughts about the past (either how good or how lousy we think it was) or the future (our hopes and dreams that things will get better), may disrupt present–tense awareness and may thwart potential encounters with our experiences. We must become comfortable with spending time "thoughtlessly" while in Nature. To "be," instead of to "think," that must become our goal.

The following exercise, in addition to fostering present– tense awareness, encourages mental discipline that will help us remain calm and centered during the meditation exercises presented in the chapter on living deliberately. It also helps keep our minds centered upon our present experience to avoid mindless encounters with our past or our future. Finally, this exercise will help keep our attention centered upon Nature as we perform the other exercises that follow.

1. Make it a part of your daily routine to spend at least five minutes actively exploring a natural object. Sunsets, flowers, trees, rocks, seashells, and other aspects of Nature are good places to begin. Use the same object for the entire five minutes. To facilitate concentration, find a time and a place that are quiet and free of distractions to practice the exercise. Do not be discouraged if your mind wanders a bit at first. Refer to the relaxation and meditation activities presented earlier for additional assistance. Remember, this activity needs to become a daily

experience for us, if we desire to re–ally ourselves with Nature.

2. Focus your full attention upon the item you have selected. Explore its details using as many of your senses as possible (feel it, smell it, taste it, hear it, as well as see it). Use your senses as your primary means to explore the item and avoid trying to "think" about it. Also, refrain from using your imagination to explore the object (imagining how it might look as a lamp, wondering how it might feel about you, and imagining how it would look if it became larger are examples of imaginative thinking which should be avoided). Stay focused upon your immediate sensory impressions of the object!

3. Once you have finished exploring your object with present–tense awareness, write down your observations and impressions. Note both what you observed about the object itself and your impressions of the encounter with it. Reflect upon your feelings of spending time engaged in present–tense awareness. Providing ourselves with immediate feedback from our encounters with Nature strengthens our alliance with her energies.

4. If your mind wanders away from your subject during the exercise, immediately refocus it on the subject. This is much like learning to ride a bicycle. At first you had to think about what you were doing. Later you realized this was no longer necessary. Through time, you will learn to stay in the present–tense without much difficulty or without even thinking about it. Thoreau, Van Gogh, Wagner, and many other great minds knew present–tense encounters with Nature stimulated their creative potential and united them with the spiritual essence present within Nature.

EXPERIMENT THREE: LIBERATE YOUR PERCEPTION —TURN ON YOUR "KLEEVISION"

"All things in this world must be seen with youthful, hopeful eyes."

Thoreau, *Journals*

If we shackle our perception of Nature with routine modes of awareness, then it will be most difficult, if not altogether impossible, to re–ally ourselves with Nature— *even if we spend considerable time in natural surroundings.* Our hectic, overly complex lifestyle often creates "mindlessness" when we spend time in Nature. Our bodies may be in Nature seeking relief from the tensions generated by our lifestyle; however, our minds still may be attending to the demands of that lifestyle. Remember Thoreau's lament: "I feel alarmed when it happens that I have walked a mile into the woods bodily without getting there in spirit...What business have I in the woods if I am thinking of something out of the woods?" Arthur Koestler refers to this mindless condition in which we are out of contact with our surroundings as having "cataracts of perception."

Koestler's metaphorical reference to the cataracts of perception pinpoints a major problem we face regarding our ability to relate with Nature. A cataract builds up over time and its effects slowly become obvious, because the accumulation goes almost unnoticed until the cataract has reduced our vision. Likewise, the layers of habit and routine which we develop as we mature, in order for us to cope with the demands of the modern lifestyle, gradually accumulate until they have reduced our awareness of Nature substantially. To repeat the same actions out of habit or custom is to be controlled by—rather than to control—our actions. Fortunately, we can remove both cataracts and habitual ways of perceiving Nature.

Artist Paul Klee discovered a means to remove his own "cataracts of perception" that could have limited his awareness. The technique he developed to liberate his awareness from habit involved temporarily altering his vision. Klee often used binoculars or other types of lenses to explore potential subjects for his work. The binoculars created an altered, somewhat distorted perspective of the subject. Klee felt this altered perspective freed his mind to uncover subtle nuances about the subject that an ordinary, more routine perspective may have overlooked. These new perspectives were a fertile realm for his imagination to explore. Klee even used the technique to give his mind an occasional "stretch."

We can employ variations of Klee's technique to give us new perspectives on Nature or simply to stretch our minds. There are three primary objectives for this exercise, and you may use the variations of Klee's technique to address any of them. Use the suggested follow—up activities to stimulate additional insights. Remember, the goal is to liberate ourselves from habitual ways of seeing Nature. Once freed of these limitations, we are able to create a more meaningful relationship between ourselves and Nature.

Objectives for Using KLEEVISION

OBJECTIVE 1. To obtain fresh new perspectives for natural objects with which you are already familiar.

OBJECTIVE 2. To explore natural objects with which you are not familiar using new means of perceptual awareness.

OBJECTIVE 3. To engage in playful, open-ended perception and thinking just to keep the mind active and stimulated or simply to enjoy exploring Nature through playful, imaginative means.

Procedure for KLEEVISION

1. Use "readymade" lenses to create new perspectives of Nature.

Select a natural object such as a rock, flower, twig, etc. Try using binoculars, telescopes, camera lenses, magnifying glasses, etc. as your lenses for altering your perception. Look through both ends of the lenses. Hold the lenses at various angles. Use a variety of lenses on the camera (wide angle, telephoto, macro-focusing). Describe your observations out loud (refer to the exercise "Describe Our Loud" presented later for suggestions) while using the readymade lenses to examine Nature. Draw or write down your ideas and insights. Use the follow-up activities for additional insight.

2. "Create" lenses.

Use drinking glasses, soft drink bottles, antique glass, glass bricks, etc. Use images reflected by objects such as stainless steel mixing bowls, aluminum foil, concave or convex mirrors, or any other reflective surface. A little distortion actually helps liberate perception!

FOLLOW UP: Extending your insights

1. Try verbalizing out loud during your observations. Describe both the object and your own feelings about the experience. If you are not familiar with the technique of verbalizing your experiences out loud, refer to experiment number six presented later in this chapter.

2. Write about the experience. What ideas, impressions, or images came to you as you engaged your KLEEVISION? What new perspectives or associations did you discover about the subject? You may wish to record them in your journal immediately and refer to them later for evaluation.

3. Draw your ideas. Create whatever images or impressions seemed to be interesting or caught your attention. You may draw either the object itself as you experienced it through KLEEVISION or your impression of it. In other words, your drawing may depict the object in a literal or representational fashion or be an abstract impression of your experience of it.

4. Take photographs of the object using your "new eyes." Try focusing through your altering lens and capture the altered image on film for later exploration. As an alternative, photograph your *impression* of the object (create on film an abstract image which, to you, expresses how you "feel" about the object).

5. Create music or a dance based upon the new perspectives. Use body movements to reflect your impressions of the object itself or of your subjective feelings about it. Another kinesthetic activity to promote understanding of your experience is to mold your impressions or ideas in clay or Play–Doh. Use any other means you feel is appropriate. KLEEVISION can stimulate many fresh perceptions for natural objects that we often take for granted.

EXPERIMENT FOUR: EXPAND AWARENESS OF NATURE THROUGH SOUND, SMELL, AND TOUCH

"I must walk more with my senses free! I must let my senses wander!"

Thoreau, *Journals*

"My profession is always to be alert, to find God in Nature, to know God's lurking places, to attend to all the oratorios and operas in Nature."

Thoreau, *Letter to Ralph Waldo Emerson*

Cultivate Awareness of Natural Rhythms and Phenomena

Seek out natural rhythms and energy patterns (sunrise and sunset, weather conditions, flowing water, animal movements or feeding patterns, etc.) in the environment and try to "become one" with them. In other words, experience these natural rhythms through the unlimited power of your imagination. Imagine what the sun feels like as it creeps up over the distant horizon, how a beam of sunlight feels throughout its eight–minute journey to the earth, or how a earthworm feels as it tunnels through the earth beneath your feet. Spending time observing various natural phenomena will facilitate an imaginative participation in the flow of life. Record any insights you receive from these imaginative encounters and incorporate them into your life. Also, draw, paint, create stories about, etc. your impressions. Acting upon the impressions you generate provides feedback that helps re–ally ourselves with Nature.

Sound and Smell to Enhance Awareness

- Listen to **animal "music."** Find ranges of meaning and subtle distinctions in a cat's meow, a dog's bark, a bird's song, a snail's trudging through the grass, a rabbit's munching, etc. You may want to use a tape recorder to collect sound specimens for later enjoyment and exploration.

- Create a **sound history** of a natural area. 1) Visit the same area on several different days and note the sounds you encounter on those occasions. 2) Visit the area during the same day, but at different times and note the various sounds. As above, you may want to use a tape recorder to collect sound specimens for later exploration. Also, try closing your eyes and noticing any differences this makes in either of the two scenarios above. Record your observations and impressions in your journal. Occasionally repeat your sound histories in these areas to notice if changes have occurred.

- Create a **smell history** of a natural area using the suggestions above.

- Create a **sound map** of a natural area such as a forest, pond, or meadow. Walk around the area being fully attentive to the natural sounds you experience. Draw a map as you walk noting the location of various sounds.

- Create a **smell map** of a natural area using the suggestions above.

- Take a **vow of silence** with your voice for a few hours when you are in Nature. Make only "musical" sounds such as wind whistling through the trees or the songs of frogs at dusk. Create your responses to Nature in "musical fashion" (however you define that term) for the duration of your vow.

- Go to a natural area where you can make "friendly" sounds to accompany natural events such as a sunset, a breeze blowing through a flower–filled meadow, the winter's first frost, etc. Be open to what Native Americans refer to as "the spirit of the place" and join with the chorus of Nature in your own unique ways as you express through sound your own impression of these natural events. Use whatever sounds you feel are appropriate.

Sense of Touch to Enhance Awareness

- Go with a friend to a comfortable natural area. Take turns blindfolding and serving as a guide for each other. When blindfolded, use your sense of touch to explore natural objects around you for ten to fifteen minutes. Keep your eyes blindfolded for the entire period to enhance your sense of touch. When you are finished, jot down your immediate impressions. Take turns with your friend using this activity.

- Go to a natural area and find twenty to thirty small natural objects such as twigs, pine cones, rocks, bark, etc. Remember, please do not disturb life forms or intrude in Nature. Once you have your objects, arrange them according to some natural quality you wish to explore such as texture or surface features, color, size, density, age, etc. For example, if you wanted to explore coarseness (texture), then place the least coarse item on your left and the most coarse on your right with the other items placed according to these two "extremes." Once you have finished, record your observations and impressions in your journal. Repeat the activity blindfolded or close your eyes as you explore the natural objects.

- Other suggestions: Try wearing socks on your hands as you explore natural objects. Use your elbow to feel the grass or your toes to feel a tree's bark, etc. Get the idea? Open up to playful, imaginative ways to explore the world around you. Observe the impact of these explorations upon your relationship with Nature.

Go on a Barefoot Walk

Sometimes we rush through Nature at the same hectic pace at which we rush to work, to the bank, to the cleaners, or to the other activities of our modern lifestyle. In our haste, we often miss Nature's subtle rhythms and nuances that would be a vital asset in re–allying ourselves with the natural world. One way to slow down our rush through Nature so that we may "encounter" Nature and experience ourselves as an integral part of our surroundings is to take a barefoot walk. Thoreau often ditched his shoes so that he could leisurely saunter through the woods and feel himself to be one with his surroundings.

This activity's goal is that we alter our routine experience of Nature which will help us devote more attention to our immediate surroundings. As you walk barefoot through Nature, pay close attention with every step to what your feet tell you about your surroundings. If your mind wanders away from your surroundings at any time during the walk, immediately refocus your attention upon what your feet feel *at that moment*. Once you have "grounded" yourself again in your immediate experience, continue the walk. Occasionally, stop for a moment, and jot down your immediate impressions. After you have finished the walk, make notes of your experience and any insights you have gained. Suggestions for taking barefoot walks include:

- Take a barefoot walk around your yard. "Feel" your way with your bare feet as you move slowly through various areas of your yard. You also may take a blindfolded walk (led by a friend, of course) through your yard and note the differences between the two experiences.

- Take a barefoot walk in a park.

- Take a barefoot walk in the woods.

- Take a barefoot walk in a stream.

- Take a barefoot walk in a meadow or pasture.

EXPERIMENT FIVE: NURTURE SYNESTHETIC AWARENESS

"This is a delicious evening, when the whole body is one sense, and imbibes delight through every pore."

Thoreau, *Walden*

What do you think the following lines may have in common?

The dawn comes like thunder.

Rudyard Kipling

Sunlight above roars like a vast invisible sea.

Conrad Aiken

A soft glowing light like lulled music.

Percy Bysshe Shelley

The murmur of the grey twilight.

Edgar Allan Poe

The quiet coloured end of evening.

Robert Browning

Did you notice that each statement expresses the sun in a *synesthetic* fashion? By definition, synesthesia is "sensory crossover," a state of awareness in which one sensory input triggers altogether different sensory responses. The quotations above describe the sun as if the authors "heard" sounds during their visual experience (sight triggers hearing). Another example of synesthesia would be how the sound of a babbling brook may "feel" as if it were massaging our body (hearing triggers touch). Because it blends our sensory input into a whole that is greater than the sum of its parts, synesthesia transcends ordinary awareness of Nature. Consider the following lines from William Blake.

If the doors of perception were cleansed,
everything would appear to man as it is, infinite.
For man has closed himself up, till he sees all
things through narrow chinks of his cavern.

Blake laments that we ordinarily process each sensory perception as if it were just a narrow chink of the whole—isolated and walled off from other senses. While watching a sunset we may see the beautiful colors and miss the synesthetic experience altogether (i.e., the sounds, smells, touch, and taste the sunset's colors could trigger in our awareness). You may be wondering: "What is wrong with just seeing the colors?" Without synesthetic awareness, we diminish the contextual basis for our experience of Nature. We also may lose contact with Nature's extraordinary subtlety. If we remain oblivious to the subtlety and contextual basis of Nature, then we certainly will thwart our efforts to establish a more intimate relationship with the world around us.

Researchers note that while virtually all young children exhibit synesthetic awareness, less than 10% of adults experience it. It is no coincidence that adults who experience synesthetic awareness are among society's most creative people—our poets, artists, musicians, writers, etc. This finding indicates that synesthesia is probably an ability to relate with Nature that many people lose during maturation. Fortunately, we can rekindle our innate capability for synesthetic, multi-sensory awareness of Nature. As you may have guessed, Thoreau's writings reveal that he had exceptional synesthetic awareness, no doubt nurtured through his intimate relationship with Nature. If we nurture synesthetic awareness, we will broaden our appreciation for the natural world. This will assist our efforts to re–ally ourselves with Nature. Let the following exercises be a starting point.

> **NOTE**: Developing synesthetic awareness may take considerable time and effort. For many of us, our synesthetic awareness has atrophied substantially since our childhood. We, therefore, should not expect immediate results. *Please be patient!*

Preliminary Exercises

1. **Use Nature's Symphony:** Go to a natural location and listen for a few minutes to the "symphony" around you. Sit still and just listen without trying to analyze the

experience—just "be" there. Also, remember that sound falls on the entire body, not just the eardrums; therefore, let your whole body "experience" the sounds. As you continue listening, be open to *whatever* impressions you experience without judging or criticizing them.

At first, focus upon each sense individually. The sense of touch is a good starting place. Select one sound from the "symphony" and imagine the "touch" of that sound upon your whole body and then upon different body parts. For example, you may try to imagine the "touch" of a bird's song upon your whole body and then upon your toes, knees, head, etc. Once you feel comfortable with this level of the activity, try listening to several sounds simultaneously and imagine their combined "touch" upon the body and its parts.

You also may involve your other senses. What sound is the most maroon? Amber? How does any particular sound or combination of sounds smell? Does a robin's song taste more chocolate than a mockingbird's? Use your imagination to create ways to experience the sounds in synesthetic fashion. Remember, there are no *right* or *wrong* ways to experience Nature. Whatever you experience is valid, because it is *your* experience! Record your impressions and observations in your journal.

2. **Using Colors:** Colors are very stimulating to the eyes and can be equally stimulating to the other senses as well. Go to a comfortable place in Nature and find a colorful item that interests you. Pick one color and explore it using the ideas below and similar ideas:

   • How does the color sound? (e.g., loud, jazzy, serene, piquant, etc.)

- What smell does it have? (citrus, pungent, earthy, aromatic, etc.)

- What would it feel like to your touch?

- What taste does it bring to mind?

3. Using Taste: Taste also makes an excellent candidate for stimulating synesthetic awareness. Select a natural item that you know is safe to taste (honeysuckle dew, pine needles, rose, chrysanthemum or nasturtium petals, clover, etc.). Ask yourself questions similar to the ones above as you experience the taste. Be open to whatever associations and impressions you experience.

4. Synesthetic Scavenger Hunt: This activity is similar to the traditional scavenger hunt except participants hunt for synesthetic experiences instead of unusual objects. Participants receive a list containing examples of synesthetic experiences similar to the suggestions below. If you use this activity alone, you could make up your own list or have a friend make one for you. Participants search in Nature for each of the items and use their imagination as a guide. Remember, there are no right or wrong answers for these experiences; *it is each person's experience that matters*. Have people describe why they had particular experiences to heighten awareness of synesthesia.

Suggestions include:

- Something that smells finicky
- A texture that sounds outrageous
- Something that smells anxious
- Something that tastes like corduroy
- A sound that tastes red

- Something that feels loud
- A sound that is green
- A smell that is gray
- Something that tastes joyful
- A texture that is orange
- A sound that is three–feet long
- A sound that is caramel
- Something that smells like truth
- Something that looks like honor

Advanced Synesthetic Exercises

1. **Sounds into Visuals**: Select an interesting sound while in Nature. Then draw, paint, mold in clay, or photograph it. How would that sound look, remembering that you can depict it abstractly (i.e., your "impression" of it as opposed to a more literal picture of it). Think how you might visually depict the nightingale's song, the gurgle of a mountain stream, or the sound made by a snowball as it hits something. Use your imagination to depict how the sound "looks" or "feels" to you, remembering that there are no *right* or *wrong* ways to express your impressions of these sounds. Be open to your hunches and impressions!

2. **Other Senses into Visuals**: Use the ideas above and the suggestions below to transform other sensory input into visual expressions. Remember, avoid depicting the sensory input's source (for example, what a smell's source "looks" like). Create visual expressions to illustrate:

   - how the yellow-orange of a monarch butterfly tastes, sounds, smells

- how springtime smells, tastes, or feels to the touch
- how a flower sounds or feels to the touch.

EXPERIMENT SIX: VERBALIZE OUT LOUD

"Scenery, when it is truly seen, reacts upon the life of the seer."

Thoreau, *Journals*

A formidable barrier to re–allying ourselves with Nature is that, in our rush to "get ahead" in life, we may assume that we already know what we will encounter in the world. If we have a busy schedule and feel that we already know what to expect as we experience Nature, then we probably will not take the time to "encounter" our surroundings. Not stopping to smell the roses because we're rushed and already know how roses smell may be an efficient way to move through life. It is not, however, the appropriate way to re–ally ourselves with Nature.

Fortunately, there are techniques to help us overcome this barrier. Creativity researcher Rosemary Gaymer feels that present–tense, highly focused awareness is not a talent reserved only for a few creative souls such as Thoreau. Rather, she believes it to be a skill that anyone can learn—*if he or she will expend the effort*. A primary way to stimulate present–tense awareness of Nature is to describe **out loud** any natural objects that interest you. Verbalizing your immediate impressions focuses your awareness and facilitates having an encounter with the natural object. Active encounters with natural objects is an important element of our efforts to re–ally ourselves with Nature.

Win Wenger's creativity research suggests that verbalization methods can contribute to our re–alliance with Nature. He has found that if we "describe the dickens" out of an object while we observe it, we will more likely "encounter" the object. As we describe an object out loud, initially we will verbalize the familiar, routine terms (pretty, colorful, interesting, spectacular, etc.) that our ordinary awareness uses to describe its experience. If we continue to describe the object out loud, we soon will run out of these familiar descriptions. At that point—*if we expend the effort to persist*—we likely will transcend an ordinary experience of the object and create an encounter with it. Then, because we have nurtured present–tense awareness, even what we consider to be the most mundane natural objects can stimulate an intimate relationship with Nature.

Procedure

1. Initially, select an object from Nature in which you have a strong interest and place it in front of you. For a minimum of five minutes describe the object **out loud**. Do not judge or censor your thoughts; say whatever comes to mind. In other words, allow your "stream of consciousness" (your immediate, uncensored thoughts and impressions) to emerge. If you run into difficulty—*do not stop*—but continue to describe the object out loud. Reaching new perspectives requires that we press onwards when we have reached the limits of ordinary awareness. (In jogging, remember, the first mile or so does not provide as much benefit as the last mile or so).

2. You may wish to describe the object to a partner or tape recorder. This allows you to receive feedback. Pay attention to the descriptions you use and notice if you shift from the descriptive terms characteristic of ordinary awareness (big, brightly colored, pretty, etc.) to more metaphorical and imaginative descriptions (a pattern resembling a railroad yard, it smells like humor would smell, etc.) characteristic of an enriched awareness.

3. When you finish, record in your journal any new insights or perspectives that you may have generated. Describe out loud the same object on different occasions and note any new ideas that may emerge.

EXPERIMENT SEVEN: LET NATIVE AMERICAN WISDOM GUIDE YOU

> "We would not always be soothing and taming nature, breaking the horse and ox, but sometimes ride the horse wild...(such was) the Indian's intercourse with nature."
>
> Thoreau, *A Week...*

Long before the European materialistic/scientific mindset with its characteristic separation of humanity from Nature had set foot in the "new world," there were many people already here living in harmony and balance with Nature. Native Americans experienced Nature as a spirit–filled entity of which they were merely a part, not as being lord and master over Nature as did the Europeans. One of the most eloquent testaments to Native American's relationship with Nature comes from Chief Seattle, who in his response to President Franklin Pierce's offer to buy the land on which his people lived, made the following statements:

> Every part of the earth is sacred to my people. Every shining pine needle, every sandy shore, every mist in the dark woods, every clearing and humming insect

is holy in the memory and experience of my people....We are part of the earth, and it is part of us. The perfumed flowers are our sisters; the deer, the horse, the great eagle, these are our brothers. The rocky crests, the juices in the meadow, the body heat of the pony, and man all belong to the same family.

Thoreau, who felt akin to the Native American experience of Nature in many ways, often revealed an awe at their ability to glean necessities from the earth without disturbing the delicate web of life around them. He also respected their awareness of a "Great Spirit" which permeates and sustains all Nature. We, too, can be awed by their alliance with Nature and let it be our guide as we seek to re–ally ourselves with Nature.

1. Native American's Chants, Prayers, and Songs

> "A prayer is just a way of becoming really conscious, really tuning in to all the relationships of everything in existence."
>
> Sun Bear
> *The Bear Tribe's Self–reliance Book*

The idea that words contain "power" to make things happen is an ancient idea that has surfaced in ancient Greece, Egypt, India, Africa, and throughout the Americas. Wherever it has appeared, people realized that there is a strong connection between human activities such as speech and natural events that occur around them. Emerson, in his book *Nature* that helped kindle the American Transcendentalist movement, suggests that as we go back through time to the origins of language, we will find that language actually emerged from ancient humanity's spiritual connection with Nature. Words themselves, he says, began as ways to express natural events and relationships and are, therefore, directly linked to the reality they describe. This is especially true among people such as Native Americans who still experience the link between words and Nature.

Native Americans used their language as a powerful "tool" to strengthen their alliance with Nature. Their chants, prayers, and songs invoked the link between words and Nature. They regarded the ability to recite these messages during life's activities as a form of wealth. (Remember, according to Holmes, wealth is a state of Mind concerning spiritual energy, not the sum of one's possessions). For example, Native Americans used these messages to ensure an abundant harvest, to heal the sick, and even to help the sun rise in the morning. If we explore their chants, prayers, and songs with a reverent and open mind, we can strengthen our own ties with Nature. Before beginning to use these methods, please consider the following suggestions.

Preliminary Suggestions

1. These chants, prayers, and songs were means of allying Native Americans with the powerful spiritual energies around them. As such, we must maintain reverence for their beliefs as we read their words. Before reading these messages, you may want to clear your mind of any distracting thoughts through meditation.

2. You may read Native American messages as part of your inspirational readings. Their natural beauty and simple wisdom can be a significant source of insight. Read only a few selections at a time and record your insights. Periodically re–read various selections to give you more perspective. Integrate your insights into your daily activities. Always give thanks to the spiritual energies around you when you receive an insight or when you experience a spiritual link between yourself and Nature. To Native Americans, giving thanks for whatever we receive in life was vital to living in harmony with Nature and her spiritual energies.

3. You also may use these messages as a source of inspiration while you perform other activities to re–ally yourself with Nature. For example, before taking a barefoot walk, read a few selections to prepare your mind. Believe that you are aligning yourself with the spiritual energies around you and feel your connection with Nature as you perform the activity. After completing the activity, record any insights or perspectives that are related to the selections you used for preparation.

4. You may use a particular chant, prayer, or song in the purpose for which it was created. For example, the "Prayer for the Deceased" used by the Omaha people is a beautiful way to say farewell to a loved one.

5. You may want to attend workshops or programs conducted by Native Americans that are designed to deepen your connections with Nature.

Native American Chants, Prayers, & Songs

Lakota: Sunrise Greeting Song

Here am I. Behold me. I am the sun. Behold me.

Kagaba: Song of Mother Earth

The mother of our songs, the mother of all our seed,
   who bore us in the beginning of things.
To our mother alone do we belong.

Oglala Sioux: Sunrise Prayer from the Inipi Purification Rite

O Morning Star, here at the place where the sun comes up; O You who have the wisdom which we seek, that our generations to come will have Light as they walk the sacred path. You lead the dawn as it walks forth, and also the day which follows with its Light which is knowledge; this You do for us and all the people of the earth, that they may see clearly in walking the wakan path; that they may know all that is holy, and that they may increase in a sacred manner.

Oglala Sioux: Prayer for Mother Earth

O Mother Earth, you are the earthly source of all existence. The fruits which you bear
are the source of life for the Earth peoples. You are always watching over your fruits as
does a mother. May the steps we take in life upon you be sacred and not weak.

Navajo: Walking Meditation

With beauty before me, may I walk
With beauty behind me, may I walk
With beauty above me, may I walk
With beauty below me, may I walk
With beauty all around me, may I walk
Wandering on a trail of beauty, lively I will walk.

Pawnee: Hako Ceremony Song

We see on Mother Earth the running streams;
We see the promise of her fruitfulness.
Truly, her power she gives us.
Our thanks to Mother Earth!

Oglala Sioux: Prayer from the Sun Dance

As I stand upon the sacred earth, upon which generations of our people have stood, I send a voice to You by offering this pipe. Behold me, O *Wakan–Tanka* (Great Spirit), for I represent all the people. Within this pipe I shall place the four Powers and all the wingeds of the universe; together with all these, who shall become one, I send a voice to You. Behold me! Enlighten my mind with Your never fading Light!

Navajo: Song for Mother Earth

The earth, its life am I
The earth, its body is my body
The earth, its thoughts are my thoughts
The earth, its speech is my speech.

Maya: Prayer Before Working the Soil

O God, my mother, my father, lord of the hills, lord of the valleys, lord of the forest, be patient with me. I am now about to do as has always been done.

Now I make you an offering, that you may be forewarned: I am about to molest your heart. Perhaps you will have the strength to endure it.

I am going to dirty you, I am going to work you in order that I may live. With all my heart I am going to work you.

Arapaho: Prayer Before Eating

All the animals above the ground, listen to me.
Animals above ground, and water animals, listen to me.
We shall eat your remnants of food.
Let them be good.
Let there be good breath and long life.

Let the people increase, the children of all ages, the girls
and the boys, and the men and women of all ages.
The food will give us strength whenever the sun runs.
Listen to us Father, Grandfather, we ask thought, heart,
love, happiness.
We are going to eat.

Lenape (Delaware): New Year Big House Ceremonial Prayer

We thank our Mother, the Earth, whom we claim as
mother because the Earth carries us and everything we
need.

Oglala Sioux: Prayer at Sunrise from The Sun Dance Ceremony

The light of Wakan–Tanka (the Great Spirit) is upon my
people;
It is making the whole earth bright.
My people are now happy!
All beings that move are rejoicing!

Omaha Prayer for the Deceased

Naked you came from Earth the Mother. Naked you
return to her. May a good wind be your road.

Native American Practices Continued

2. Participate in Native American Rituals

"A ritual can be defined as an enactment of a
myth. By participating in a ritual, you are
actually experiencing a mythological life. And
it's out of that participation that one can learn
to live spiritually."

Joseph Campbell, *The Power of Myth*

Native Americans, as well as many other people around the world, use rituals to enhance their participation in the harmony and balance of Nature. They join their energies with Nature's energies to expand their spiritual awareness and to participate more fully and harmoniously in the natural world. If we perform their rituals with reverence, we can experience greater oneness with Nature and a sense of harmony in all that we do. Use the following simple rituals to help re–ally yourself with Nature. You also can learn other Native American rituals from experienced teachers.

Pueblo Sunrise Ritual

Carl Jung found the Pueblo people of the American Southwest practicing an ancient ritual in which they prayed each morning to help the sun rise in the Eastern sky and to lift the world from darkness. Jung was intrigued by their continued performance of the ritual long after they had been told by "science" that the sun only appears to rise in the sky, because the earth rotates on its axis. To the Pueblo people, scientific explanations were no substitute for their experience of Nature. They felt themselves to be an integral part of Nature's activities and believed that their prayers actually assisted the sun to rise each day.

1. If you wish to join in celebrating their ritual, arise before dawn. Relax and clear your mind. Begin to pray to the sun for its arrival. You may use the Native American prayers in the preceding activity or find your own.

2. Allow your mind to feel the sun as the source of light on earth. Feel yourself connected with its energies and ask it to bless us again with its presence. As the first rays of dawn appear, feel them as if they were spiritual energy patterns flooding you and all that is around you. Give thanks to the sun for making another appearance in the world and let joy bubble up from deep within your being.

3. As the sun continues to rise and the sky becomes filled with its radiance, experience how trees, grasses, flowers, birds, horses, and all other life forms around you celebrate the sun's return. Feel yourself as a part of Nature's celebration of another day's arrival.

4. When you have finished, prepare for your daily activities. Whenever possible throughout the day, reflect upon your prayers and your experiences with the sunrise ritual. Feel your participation in Nature's activities and give thanks for this awareness.

Cherokee Tree Ritual

> When you walk in the mountains stands of cedar, among the wise old elder trees, anything you want to know you can find there.
>
> Saying of the Lummi Tribe of Puget Sound

Many Native American people have a tree ritual in which they seek guidance from a particular tree or group of trees. To them, a tree is a wise spiritual entity whose wisdom comes from several directions: it is long–lived and has experienced many things, it is sturdy, it balanced because it is of both the air (Father Sky) and of the earth (Mother Earth), it is strong–yet it is flexible, and it provides resources for many other plant or animal species. Native Americans conduct a ceremonial ritual in which they ask the selected tree several questions, and they receive a reply to each question. After they receive insight, they thank the tree for its assistance and offer it some cornmeal or tobacco as a gesture of appreciation (a giveaway). The ritual that follows has been adapted from the Cherokee People. It is a powerful way to unite your life and its issues with that of Nature.

Preliminary Suggestions:

- Conduct the ceremony upon a special event or occasion (birthday, holiday, full moon, change in life circumstance, etc.) or whenever you feel the need to seek guidance.

- Select a tree for the ceremony either by letting it "call out" to you and lead you to it or by selecting it for its beauty, strength, and spiritual presence.

- Direct one question towards each of the four compass directions (N/S/E/W). To Native Americans, each of the four directions has a spiritual significance. To show appreciation for the tree's assistance with your needs, you will offer the tree a small amount of cornmeal or tobacco after receiving each answer. Reverently and lovingly place the offering at the tree's base. For example, when asking a question at the North position, place the offering near the North side of the tree's trunk, etc.

- Ask the questions and wait patiently for a response. Your response may be a inner impression or image, an external image or symbol (a vision), an inner voice or intuition, or an external audible voice. Be patient and let the tree answer in its own manner. Be open to whatever insight you receive.

- Stand with your back gently resting against the tree as you move to each of the four directions of the compass. Before asking a question, relax for a moment and settle your mind. Become one with the tree and with the moment.

After asking each question, wait for a reply. Remember, you may see, feel, hear, or get an inner sensing of it.

The Questions:

1. Face SOUTH and ask the tree: "Who am I?"

2. Face NORTH and ask: "What is my purpose?"

3. Face WEST and ask: "Where did I come from?"

4. Face EAST and ask: Where am I going?"

5. Go to the direction in which you received the most "powerful" or "stimulating" answer. Place your forehead against the tree. Give to the tree anything (a problem, a limiting thought, a fear, etc.) you wish to let go of at this time. Thank the tree for sharing its wisdom with you and for taking what you have left with it. Hug the tree and offer it more cornmeal or tobacco. You may wish to stand back from the tree and spend a few minutes in humble appreciation for what the tree means both to you and to Nature.

Seneca People's "Four Questions" Ritual

The Seneca people of the Northeast have a ritual to help them walk in harmony and balance with Nature as they perform certain activities. For example, if they need guidance in helping young members of the group prepare for initiation, each person would ask him or herself four questions to stimulate insight into the situation. To the Seneca, as well as to many other Native American people, the number four carries spiritual significance. The answers to the four questions, therefore, would provide valuable insights which could guide them in their activities and let them walk in harmony with Nature. Whenever you need to align your daily activities more intimately with Nature, use the Seneca People's Four Questions as a guide.

- If you need guidance to ensure that your actions are harmonious with Nature, ask yourself the following questions used by the Senecas:

   1. Am I happy with what I am doing now?

   2. Is what I am doing adding to the confusion?

   3. What am I doing to further peace and contentment?

   4. How will I be remembered for this activity after I am gone, in absence or in death?

- Reflect upon your answers. Allow your mind to provide insights that may guide you along a path that meets your genuine needs without harming Nature or others.

3. Iroquois "Seven Generation Rule"

One of the most simple, yet effective, ways we can re–ally ourselves with Nature comes from the Iroquois people of the Northeast. Anytime the Iroquois opened their tribal meetings, they began with a joint proclamation: "In our deliberation, we must consider the impact of our decisions on the next seven generations." This proclamation bound them to consider not only their immediate needs when making decisions, but also the needs of all lifeforms who would live during the next 150 to 200 years. To the Iroquois, satisfying their short–term needs could never outweigh the needs of future generations. And since they perceived that all other lifeforms were their equals within Nature's web of life, paying attention to the needs of coming generations also meant respecting other lifeforms' needs.

Imagine for a moment that modern societies adopted the Iroquois proclamation as a model for decision–making. We would understand that buying nonrecyclable or toxic-laden products causes the entire web of life to exist upon a landscape strewn with over–crowded landfills and toxic waste dumps. We would understand that generating nuclear power to feed our energy–squandering "modern conveniences" will poison countless lifeforms, both human and nonhuman, yet to be born. We also may see the futility of using material objects to fill our inner spiritual void. The Iroquois have shown us that it is possible to ally ourselves with Nature by "thinking before we act." Use the following suggestions to adapt their method to your own needs.

> **In our deliberation, we must consider the impact of our decisions on the next seven generations.**

Use the Iroquois Proclamation to guide your decision:

- when you are considering a major purchase (home, car, appliance, furniture, etc.)

- when you are making career decisions

- when you are considering investment decisions

- when you plan to spend time in Nature (camping, hiking, gardening, relaxing, etc.)

- when you are considering how to dispose of something

- whenever you feel that a potential decision might impact Nature or future generations.

Bibliography and Resources

Primary Resource

The Writings of Henry David Thoreau, edited by Bradford Torrey and Francis Allen, Boston: Houghton Mifflin, 1906

Additional Resources

Joseph Epes Brown, *The Spiritual Legacy of the American Indian*, New York: Crossroads Publishing, 1982

Edward Waldo Emerson, *Henry Thoreau as Remembered by a Young Friend*, Boston: Riverside Press, 1917

Ralph Waldo Emerson, *Essays and Journals*, Atlanta: The Programmed Classics/ Nelson Doubleday, 1968

Walter Harding, *The Days of Henry Thoreau*, New York: Alfred A. Knopf, 1965

John Hicks, ed., *Thoreau in Our Season*, U.Mass., 1962

Ernest Holmes, *The Science of Mind*, New York: Putnam's, 1988 (Fiftieth Anniversary Edition)

Lewis Mumford, *The Brown Decades*, New York: Harcourt, Brace & Company, 1931

Winfred E. Nagley, "Thoreau on Attachment" in *Philosophy East and West,* January, 1954, pages 307-320

Sherman Paul, *The Shores of America: Thoreau's Inward Exploration*, Urbana: University of Illinois Press, 1958

Robert Richardson, *Henry Thoreau, A Life of the Mind*, Berkeley: University of California Press, 1986

Robert Sayre, *Thoreau and the American Indian*, Princeton: Princeton University Press, 1977

Sun Bear, *The Bear Tribe's Self–reliance Book*, New York: Prentice Hall, 1988

NOTE: A few experiments contained in this book have been adapted from the author's other book, *Secrets from Great Minds,* to apply to the specific needs of people seeking to live more deliberately and to re–ally themselves with Nature.

— ABOUT THE AUTHOR —

Dr. John McMurphy has spent the past fifteen years in a search for "Secrets from Great Minds," the universal wisdom from Eastern and Western cultures that assisted great minds in attaining their highest mental and spiritual potential. He has "field–tested" his experiments in living more deliberately adapted from Thoreau, other great minds, and Native Americans with a wide variety of people and has found considerable success in helping people to develop their innate creative potential. His clients include:

- Southwestern Bell   • Boston Society of Architects

- First Tennessee Bank   • The American Red Cross

- Southern Methodist University, University of Texas, Texas Christian University, University of Louisville, and Saint Xavier University Continuing Education Programs

- The Walden Institute Human Potential Resource Center

- Spiritual organizations throughout the U.S. and Canada

Other books and materials by the author:

Books: *Secrets from Great Minds*   (ISBN 0–9635487–9–4)

         Speaking of Mother Earth   (ISBN 0–9635487–7–8)
         (Coming in Spring 1994)

Audiotapes of Presentations:

- Carl Jung — The Undiscovered Self

- The Cosmic Christ   • Lao Tzu and Taoism

- Native American Spiritual Traditions—Hopi & Navajo

- The Mystical Einstein

- Unleashing the Mind's Full Potential

To receive information on these or other publications, please call John McMurphy at (800) 321–2760.